MARKETING
FOR THE
MENTAL HEALTH
PROFESSIONAL

MARKETING
FOR THE
MENTAL HEALTH
PROFESSIONAL

An Innovative Guide for Practitioners

DAVID P. DIANA

WILEY

John Wiley & Sons, Inc.

Library of Congress Cataloging-in-Publication Data:

Diana, David P.

Marketing for the mental health professional : an innovative guide for practitioners / David P. Diana.

p. ; cm.

Includes bibliographical references and index.

Summary: "There are a few available training programs on the practical aspects of succeeding
in the mental health profession for mental health professionals. Marketing for the Mental Health
Professional provides powerful, proven sales and marketing techniques as well as strategies to achieve
high quality, value-based services in the mental health practice. Filled with real-life stories and helpful
tips, this book presents tools for generating better publicity, conducting a job search, understanding
the value propositions, and engaging with clients for long-term success for both new and seasoned
practitioners." — Provided by publisher.

ISBN 978-0-470-56091-4 (pbk. : alk. paper)

1. Mental health services — Marketing. I. Title.

[DNLM: 1. Mental Health Services — organization & administration. 2. Achievement.
3. Marketing of Health Services. 4. Professional-Patient Relations. WM 30 D538m 2010]

RA790.75.D53 2010

616.890068'8 — dc22

2009042887

To my wife Nicole
and
Our two sons, Ethan and Avery

Contents

CONTENTS

Preface

When we are no longer able to change a situation, we are challenged to change ourselves.

— Viktor E. Frankl (1984)

A career in mental health is rewarding and challenging, inspiring and at times discouraging, open and yet surprisingly restrictive. These dichotomies define the core of a life spent in service of the psychological and emotional well-being of others.

Since I began my mental health career in 1994 I've heard much talk about the sacrifices one makes when choosing the life of a behavioral health care provider. It is a noble endeavor indeed! However, this book is not about burdens and sacrifice. It's about innovation, opportunity, and abundance. It is also about change and about breaking free in a profession where few see how this can possibly be done.

This book honors the caretaker in you while giving equal importance to your own well-being. A career in the behavioral sciences offers a vast reservoir of opportunity, more so than at any other time in our profession's history. But those opportunities are sometimes difficult to see and hear. This book is about those untapped opportunities.

The history of our profession reveals a discipline that, since its inception, has challenged the status quo in pursuit of truth and understanding. Innovation, curiosity, a sense of wonder and growth were all bedrock principles.

But what are we to make of the mental health profession today? Are we living those bedrock principles? Are they available to us?

The material presented here will teach you how to combine your understanding of human behavior with innovative business ideas, thereby giving you the best of both worlds: financial success and the ability to do what you love. Learn from the disciplines of sales, marketing, and business development, and you will bring about new levels of success no matter what your interests or what role you choose to play in the field.

The new rules in today's economy are important not only for big business but for professionals in all walks of life including behavioral health care.

In a dynamic world, we know all too well that change is a constant. The question is never about deciding whether to change. The question is about what kind of change is needed.

I am taking you on a journey into new opportunity within the profession. It's a story about you. It's a story about the possibilities available to you.

And it is well worth the effort.

Acknowledgments

I would like to thank my mother for her editing skills. Her support of this project helped make this book what it is today.

I would also like to thank my editor at John Wiley & Sons, Marquita Flemming. I am extremely fortunate to have met her. Marquita's enthusiasm, guidance, and expertise have been invaluable and enlightening.

PART ONE

New Beginnings

CHAPTER ONE

Introduction

It was late afternoon, the conference was winding down, and I found myself in the middle of yet another discouraging conversation. A CEO for a medium sized mental health organization was talking about the state of the field and his belief that it had become virtually impossible to operate a successful business in the profession. He offered facts about insurance companies and managed care, stories about businesses that tried and failed, the lack of government support, and a general indifference on the part of communities as a whole regarding the value of mental health services.

As our discussion came to a close, he took one last breath, broadened his shoulders, and ended with a final statement: "There is simply no way to succeed. You have to be a martyr to be in this field for too long."

He was not the first person to approach me with an apocalyptic view of the profession. Throughout the entire week I heard complaint after complaint. People were frustrated, discouraged, and concerned about their future in the industry.

Over the course of my 14+ years in the mental health profession I've heard my fair share of venting and have issued my own in abundance. There can be no doubt that the mental health industry has its share of obstacles and issues. In spite of all these challenges, however, there are opportunities for growth, rewarding work, and ultimately, financial success in the industry.

This book is designed to take a closer look at specific success factors beyond helping others—the hallmark and foundation of the profession. Instead, it chooses to explore directly, and without apologies, other important elements:

- Career growth and advancement
- Organizational growth and success
- Competitive advantage and differentiation in the marketplace
- Financial success for the practitioner

This book is a practical guide for any and all mental health professionals looking to achieve long-term success in the field. Much of the information discussed will be new, however, it is important to note that many of these concepts and models are not new to other industries. In many respects we are behind the curve, and, as a result, the information presented should serve as a wake-up call of sorts for all those in the field. I say "wake-up call" simply because this book proposes a different way of thinking about the profession, one that involves leveraging and incorporating key business, sales, and marketing principles that best-in-class organizations and top performing sales/marketing professionals use to generate an increase in market share, financial wealth, and overall success.

BEGINNING THE EXPLORATION

The CEO who spoke with me about his impressions of the field is not incorrect in his attempt to describe the state of the profession. A mental health career is an honorable and courageous endeavor, which can come at a significant price. We see state governments use mental health services as a scapegoat for poor financial management and planning, choosing to balance their Medicaid books at the expense of community based mental health programs. As a result, government mental health employees are asked to serve effectively with few resources, little pay, and even fewer options to grow professionally. Mental health services in the private sector are equally challenged. Insurance companies devalue mental health treatment as evidenced by limited reimbursement rates, obscenely high deductibles, few behavioral healthcare plans for employees, and the implementation of complex and convoluted systems that test the most patient and saint-worthy of practitioners.

These are some of the realities of the industry. And yet, people do manage to achieve success in this business, whether it is finding a rewarding job that engages them, achieving financial success in private practice, or through many other ways in which we may uniquely define success.

How do they succeed? Is it merely luck of the draw? What I found with many of these people and practices was the presence and effective use of a core set of sales, marketing, and business principles that enabled them to overcome obstacles within the profession. It is the understanding and use of these principles, many of which are severely neglected or simply unknown within our field, that have helped mental health professionals succeed in a variety of ways.

This is the core message I communicate in the pages that follow. You will be presented with different philosophies, new strategies, real life stories, and very practical step-by-step guides and resources.

- If you're new to the field and looking for work, the information offered will help open doors for you.
- If you're a behavioral health care leader or executive, these concepts will add impact and relevance to your existing sales and marketing efforts.
- If you work in an organization, these principles and ideas will expand your career, increase your value, and help you move up the organizational ladder.
- If you're a seasoned private practitioner or consultant, these concepts will enable you to build on your success and position yourself for greater growth in the future.

Choose what resonates with you and make an effort to integrate it within your own professional paradigm.

CLEARING TO CREATE OPPORTUNITY

Before moving forward, let's acknowledge that we all come to the profession with our own concerns and biases. Some of these may be helpful, and some may not. As an initial step I ask that you put aside some of the old and/or negative beliefs that might prevent you from being able to adopt and leverage some of the principles and ideas discussed in this book. This is not to say these beliefs are not true. They may in fact be very real. The goal here is to silence these beliefs, at least temporarily, in the hopes of uncovering new opportunities.

Not sure what these biases might be? How do these sound for starters?

- We are in this field to help others, not to make money.
- There are so few good opportunities in the field.
- I need to take this job and pay my dues since this is how it has always been done.
- Government agencies are a losing proposition for the mental health profession.
- The profession doesn't have an effective voice at the table when it comes to federal and state legislation.
- Insurance companies regulate the industry in ways that are extremely hurtful for the overall growth and success of the profession.
- Communities, organizations, and individuals do not understand or value mental health services.

Feel free to add to the list. Write your ideas down if you must and tuck them away for another day.

All set? Great! Now let's move forward and begin learning how to gain a competitive advantage in the mental health industry.

SECRETS OF SUCCESS AND THE SALES STIGMA

"Everybody lives by selling something."

—*Robert Louis Stevenson*

The business world is changing at an incredibly fast pace, and many of these changes have a profound impact on the way people do business. Technological advances that decentralize and empower people at all levels; new concepts in sales and marketing that enable you to grow your business at hyperspeed using a sophisticated multimedia approach represent a mere fraction of the business changes and opportunities in the marketplace. Most of us in the mental health field, however, remain blissfully ignorant and unaware of these subtle but powerful events. Those lucky few who become aware of some of these changes are presented with a window of opportunity that can lead to tremendous growth and independence. Opportunities abound for those who are open to some of these new ideas and willing to integrate new concepts into their service model. The key lies in how highly skilled mental health professionals approach the marketplace and what tools they choose to use in order to succeed in a competitive environment.

A key area most mental health practitioners are sorely lacking in is the understanding and use of sophisticated sales and marketing skills. Clinicians receive heavy doses of clinical training in graduate schools and through continuing education programs. However, very little is offered in terms of how to succeed in the profession from both a financial and career development perspective. There are business seminars focusing on billing practices, business systems, and various administrative tasks; but few, if any, discuss the power and importance of sales and marketing in our profession. This area is often so untapped that adopting even some of the more basic principles will immediately distinguish you in the profession and give you a decided advantage in the mental health marketplace.

Confronting the Stigma

At first glance, the idea of adopting sales and marketing principles conjures up images of self-serving, manipulative tactics and ploys. As a result, a sales and marketing approach is often furthest from the mind of a mental health professional. This position, however, is misguided and comes from a limited understanding of sales and marketing theory and practice. First and foremost, selling and the sales process are critical elements in all areas of commerce. No business takes place without a sales transaction of some sort or another. Mental health services are not utilized unless a sale is made and someone chooses to use a specific clinical service; you are not hired into a clinical position unless you effectively sell yourself to the hiring manager; a private practice does not last long without consistent sales for services; and funding for community programs is not awarded unless a government entity is sold on the need and importance of those services.

Sales and marketing activities are a critical part of the mental health business, but before your anxiety level rises, let's understand what I mean by these two terms. As you take a closer look at each of these disciplines in the upcoming chapters you'll find that they are highly sophisticated and value driven activities perfectly suited to the mental health profession. Sales and marketing are more closely linked to the behavioral sciences than you may realize. And it is this fact that should excite you.

How could they possibly be tied to the mental health profession? In the pages to follow you will see that these two disciplines, like the field of psychology itself, concern themselves greatly with the study of human behavior. As a result, the tools, techniques, and skill sets required of both are already present in you. All you need to do is bring them to the surface.

Don't take my word for it, though. Read on and see how truly important, exciting, and fun this journey can be.

SUMMARY

- There is real opportunity for growth, advancement, and overall success within the mental health profession. Understanding and leveraging key sales, marketing, and business principles will help make these opportunities a reality for you.
- Behavioral health care organizations can significantly impact their bottom line and improve their quality of care utilizing innovative sales and marketing tools and techniques.
- Understand that you are involved in sales and marketing regardless of your profession. Resistance to this fact will only hinder your progress.
- Changes within the industry offer tremendous opportunity for those who can identify those changes and respond quickly. Technology is one area that offers much reward within the profession.
- Sales and marketing concern themselves greatly with the study of human behavior, making them an excellent fit for the mental health profession.

CHAPTER TWO

Marketing and the Mental Health Profession

A Powerful Combination

It's inevitable. Once people learn that I work in the mental health industry they begin to fire off a series of endless questions.

"So I hear you're a therapist?"

Me: *"Well, yes. I'm in the mental health profession, and I do a lot of different things."*

"Do you analyze what is going on with people all the time? Are you diagnosing everyone whenever you're in a social setting? That must be fascinating."

Sound familiar? It's not uncommon, and probably more of a nuisance than anything else. However, in my mind, this kind of interaction reveals one of the main challenges within our field today. It offers us insight into how people in our communities understand and define the world of psychology. And if we look at this type of interaction more closely, we find that it has a significant impact on how our profession is viewed in the marketplace and how we impress on people the value of our services. It is, in essence, a marketing problem.

One of the main reasons why we experience these kinds of interactions has to do with the history of psychology as a whole. Our roots are grounded within a disease-based model. And while this approach may have been essential to the development of psychology as a science, its growth within this model has also left us with some significant challenges.

Ironically, when people think of the mental health profession they aren't focusing on the "health" component. If you were to conduct a free association experiment and offer the terms *mental health* and *psychology*, chances are those terms would conjure up images of psychiatric wards much more so than health and wellness initiatives. Our emphasis on diagnostics contributes mightily to this image as it is presumed we are looking to identify what is "wrong" with someone more than anything else. The questions in this scenario provide an excellent example of this negative image. It may be disguised or couched as "fascinating," but the person is most likely suspicious or anxious about my intent. She may be asking herself, "Is he diagnosing what is wrong with me?"

You and I know that the field of psychology is about much more than disorders, disease, and the treatment of the severely ill. It's also about personal growth and creating more meaningful and happier lives. So how do we get this message across to others? How do we create a compelling message that will excite people and get them to seek out our services?

Marketing, if used effectively, helps to answer these questions, and it is here that we begin our journey.

DEMYSTIFYING THE MARKETING PROCESS

In 1997 I was an entry-level business consultant working for a team of industrial organizational psychologists. The first few months were exciting as I managed to get myself on a large project for a very big client. One day, our senior manager called a team meeting to discuss the next phase of this project.

"Steve, I'd like you to take the lead on identifying our new sales strategy and David, I want you to clarify our marketing initiatives. Sound good?"

Well, if I were being honest at the time, I would have said *"No, not so good"*! For several months prior to this meeting we worked on all sorts of sales and marketing efforts and everything seemed fine. However, when he assigned me as the marketing lead, I found myself face-to-face with a very humbling reality. I had no idea what the differences were between sales and marketing! I wasn't even sure if they were, in fact, different. It all seemed to blend together for me. Our team used these terms interchangeably. One day sending a press release was a "sales effort," the next day we called it a "marketing initiative."

So what in the world is the difference between sales and marketing? The differences can be subtle, but they are important to note.

Let's take a look at each briefly before moving on.

Sales Defined

At its core, **selling is the act of persuading or influencing a client to buy a product or service**. It is typically a one-to-one communication phenomenon, meaning you are interacting with a specific client *(individual or organization)* in an effort to have them use your services.

In mental health, if you speak with a family over the phone about your services and how you can be of help, you are engaging in the sales process. If you were to meet with the CEO of a behavioral health care organization to discuss offering

10

clinical consultation to his or her staff, that would also involve a sales process of some kind. And if you are in a job interview, your ability to convince the hiring manager that you are the best person for the job is a sales process.

Marketing Defined

Marketing, on the other hand, tends to be more strategic. **It is everything you do to reach clients and build awareness.** It's the message that prepares a potential client for a sale.

Marketing activities are designed to support sales efforts. As an example, sending out direct mailers to your target audience is a marketing effort. It's designed to build awareness and encourage people to contact you so that you are in a better position to make a sale. When you follow up with these prospective clients to see if they received the mailer you are engaging in a sales effort. You typically build awareness through marketing and then look to reap the rewards of those efforts through your direct sales activities.

Advertising, public relations, community events, business cards, web sites, brochures, and direct mailers are all forms of marketing.

But marketing has much more depth than the more traditional forms we are accustomed to seeing. Marketing is also about creating passion and connecting people. It is about relationships and conversations. Now more than ever marketing has the ability to bring people together in powerful ways, and I discuss this newer form of marketing in much greater detail and show you how to apply these principles in a mental health practice as you proceed through the book.

Old and New Marketing

With the dawn of the age of television, companies discovered a powerful process for building success: take advantage of the scarce communication resources available, and deliver as many messages possible to the general public. Television ads, radio promotions, billboards, and magazines all fit in nicely with this new model. Some experts refer to this as "Interruption Marketing." Businesses craft a message that is designed to interrupt potential customers throughout the day. Billboards on the roadways, television commercials that pop up every five minutes, and radio advertisements while you're stuck in traffic are all interruption marketing vehicles. Under this model, businesses thought little about customer need and would simply blast a message across communication channels hoping to find and convince people to buy their product.

Promote your product or service as often as possible, then take a large portion of your earnings from these promotional campaigns and put it back into more advertisements. This model worked, and it worked unbelievably well. However, it was not a game for the poor. In most cases, the biggest companies with the deepest pockets won the hearts and minds of consumers.

Businesses also began to realize that they earned the largest profits when they created average, easy to produce products that appealed to the masses. Figure 2.1 shows a traditional marketing bell curve. Businesses worked hard to offer products for consumers in the middle of the curve. They avoided the fringes such as the "early adopters" and the "late adopters" altogether. And why did they do this? Because the sweet spot of financial success could be found right in the middle of the curve with the largest consumer base.

In an effort to reach the masses, companies used (and still use) this interruption model. This quickly became the standard form of marketing, and it is one we all experience and know on a daily basis.

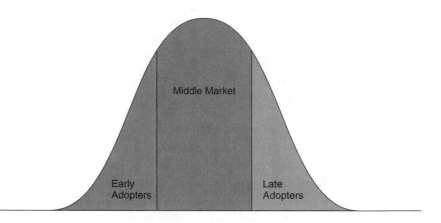

Figure 2.1 Traditional Marketing Bell Curve

What Do Old and New Marketing Have to Do with a Career in Mental Health?

Okay, so why do I tell you all this?

Because the era of traditional marketing is losing its power, and a new form of marketing is gaining significance. Market influence is no longer the direct result of the size and financial resources of a business. Today, we all have a significant amount of influence and ability to reach our clients as the power is shifting away from the few to the many.

Your understanding of this market shift will also help you to be smarter and more effective in how you choose to promote your services and yourself. If you choose to use more traditional forms of advertising, you need to know that this may not be the best solution for you. Placing an advertisement in a local newspaper may have been a great marketing strategy in the past, but it is becoming less and less so in today's marketplace. There are better and more cost-effective ways for you to make an impact and the real treasures can be found in an ever expanding and evolving approach to marketing.

EXPLORING THE NEW MARKETING MODEL

As a starting point for this discussion, let's consider some differences between the old marketing model and the new one arising today.

Older or traditional marketing is often about:

- Reach
- Control
- Company needs
- Interruption
- Domination
- Manipulation

It is focused on communicating a message and offering a service with little regard for the client's need.

Newer marketing is often about:

- Value
- Client need
- Relationships
- Community
- Permission
- Opportunity
- Sharing
- Problem solving
- Openness
- Conversations

This kind of marketing focuses on customers' needs and works to offer services and products that meet those needs as best as possible.

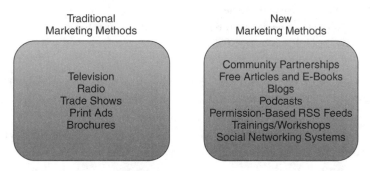

Figure 2.2   Marketing Methods

Figure 2.2 offers a snapshot of what some of these marketing approaches look like depending on the method used. I discuss many of these in the pages and chapters to follow.

Why Traditional Marketing Is Losing Its Power

When I was a boy, I was obsessed with superheroes and Disney. I thought about them constantly. However, if I wanted to watch a show about superheroes, I had to wait until Saturday morning at 8:00 to watch a 30-minute episode of *Super Friends*. It didn't matter if it was a show about Superman or a show about the Wonder Twins. It didn't even matter if they were reruns. This was my one shot every week, so by the time Saturday rolled around I was overcome with excitement and anticipation! The same can be said of Disney. I could wait for a Disney movie in the theaters, or I could watch the Disney movie that aired every Sunday evening at 7:00. I was glued to the TV no matter what Disney offered on Sunday night.

Now contrast that with my 6-year-old son today. He loves superheroes and Disney, but he's far more discerning than I ever was. Why? If my son wants to watch a superhero show, he can scan the six or seven kid's channels and find a show for every superhero imaginable. And if he doesn't like those, he can go to the recorded shows from our DVR, or he can rent a show or movie featuring whatever superhero he happens to like best that day. If he wants to watch Disney, he can turn on the Disney channel or rent a Disney movie. My son has choices and a lot of them! As a result, he's picky with what he watches. It takes a lot to get my son's attention. He isn't drowning in a sea of scarcity.

People are becoming more and more discriminating users of services and products in much the same manner as my son. And rightfully so. People are simply inundated with too much information, and since they have more and more choices, they have the power to choose what messages they are willing to let in. This helps to explain why the traditional marketing model is dwindling in power and influence. Interrupting the masses with a generic and self-serving message can be easily ignored today. People want something better. They want something that will directly benefit them.

It is this shift that serves as the tipping point for anything you choose to do in the profession.

- Do you want to get paid for a mental health workshop you deliver? How is the workshop unique? How does it meet the needs of a discriminating consumer so that he or she will pay attention?
- Do you run an intensive outpatient substance abuse program? How do you fill the group? What is the draw for people to choose you? What makes it remarkable?
- Are you attempting to start and lead a non-profit movement? How do you build a following and engage people to be active participants? Do you

use technology to build your voice? Do you offer something of incredible value to potential members so they cannot ignore you?

All these are sales and marketing questions, and they all speak to the dilemma and promise that comes from a shifting marketplace.

The new marketplace offers you many more choices and opportunities for success than have ever existed before. Technology and vast improvements in communication systems give you more influence and reach than ever before. As a result, you can get your message out to others in powerful ways and avoid the use of an expensive marketing campaign. In the upcoming chapters I present many of these tools. More importantly, I show you that they are easy and fun to use.

New Marketing Models for the Mental Health Profession

Marketing used to be mostly about advertising, but effective marketing today is about building relationships and engaging communities. It's about telling stories people want to hear, adding value through information sharing, and participating in open and honest conversations that motivate and energize people.

This is a critical point to understand. If you understand this shift on a deeper level, you will integrate these concepts into the way you operate on a professional level, and the change you create for yourself will be profound.

Let me clarify what I mean when I reference the idea of new marketing models. We have already discussed the diminishing value of a traditional marketing approach. Markets in today's economy are driven by conversations at a grassroots level. And you can participate in this process both online or offline. People are engaging in conversations and learning from one another at an incredibly fast pace. They don't have time to hear from businesses that couch their messages in marketing fluff and propaganda. Why should they spend the time when they can engage in real conversations with like-minded people who are more than willing to help them solve a problem or turn them on to a resource that might help them? A mental health practitioner who takes the time to engage people at this level will significantly improve his or her reach and influence.

Have you heard of *The ClueTrain Manifesto*? Until a few years ago I had never heard of it and for good reason. It was written by a handful of technology whizzes in the year 1999 (Levine, Locke, Searls & Weinberg). It's considered to be the seminal work of the twenty-first century for the online world. And even if technology will never be your thing, the insights it offers are important to understand as we find our footing in today's new marketplace. I highly recommend it, and you can download it for free at www.cluetrain.com.

At first glance, when you read *The ClueTrain Manifesto* it appears to be narrow in focus and fairly straightforward. On the surface it speaks to a technological revolution. However, look a little deeper, and you'll find it's packed with marketing insights and lessons for those who are willing to listen.

Because people are now given the opportunity to learn from one another through sophisticated social networks, they come to realize that they can get more of what they need from people who are an integral part of those conversations. *The ClueTrain Manifesto* predicted that these new conversations would change the way markets function. And guess what? They were right!

If your marriage is in trouble and you need help, you might engage your network of friends for the real scoop on who to turn to for help. Or, you might turn to the Internet and do some research on whether marriage counseling is worth your while. And if you happen to find a therapist in your community on the Web who is participating in an online discussion about marriage counseling, then you might choose to approach that therapist with your problem or join the online discussion.

What are you to make of this emerging marketplace? How does it possibly relate to the field of mental health? In my opinion, its message is directly applicable to the work you do. Heed its warnings, follow its advice, and you'll be more effective at marketing your services.

People are tuning out messages they see as disingenuous or stale. They don't want our standard message about the importance of counseling and how it can help. They don't want our brochure or our magazine advertisement touting the virtues of psychotherapy. They want you to back up the rhetoric with real action and value. They want something tangible and real, something that is empowering and interesting. Only then are people choosing to act.

Figure 2.3 summarizes one of the key points of *The ClueTrain Manifesto*. People are engaging in all kinds of important and smart conversations with one another. They are paying less and less attention to businesses and individuals who refuse to change their approach. Their messages are becoming largely ignored.

Reaching Out to Your Audience

How do you gain the attention of people in the community? Do you offer them the same old story about mental health, or are you truly listening to what people are saying? Are you participating in the conversation at a meaningful level so that people hear what you have to say? These were some of the

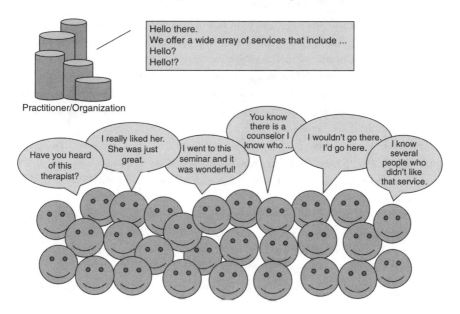

Figure 2.3 The New Marketing Model

questions I was faced with as a sales representative for a large behavioral health care organization several years ago.

Our department was tasked with filling our organization's inpatient and outpatient services. We spent our days inundating people with constant sales calls. We would try to see as many potential referral sources as possible each and every week. We would drop off brochure after brochure. At times we'd have nothing new to say, and people were tired of seeing us. At best we'd be able to leave our materials with a nurse or an assistant at a medical practice. The motto "more is better" guided our sales strategy. We approached our marketing campaign in similar fashion. We advertised wherever we could with little concern for our target market. Local newspapers, farm-league baseball teams, billboards, radio, event sponsorships, and so on. The list went on and on. But we never truly created positive change. We never really made much of an impact that would lead to better partnerships and ultimately more growth.

Then something wonderful happened. A restructuring of our department gave our team new power and influence. Our new leaders believed true power existed in building relationships and offering value to referral sources. Now the quality of our conversations far outweighed the quantity. Our focus was on finding ways to build value and to help our referral sources any way possible. We were no longer just advertising and selling, we were partnering. Suddenly, people wanted to meet with us. Doctor's offices that instituted no sales call rules created exceptions for our team. Why? Because they might be provided with a new community resource to help them, or we might be able to help them promote their practices. They welcomed us because they knew we had something important and useful to say while we were there. So while the amount of our sales calls diminished, the quality improved tremendously.

This approach is precisely what a new marketing model hopes to accomplish. Avoid approaching potential clients with a worn-out marketing approach and sales pitch. They will not hear it! Be a part of the conversation by focusing on their needs and speaking in an open and honest manner. The same approach will help you peak the interest of new clients; it will help you build more solid referral partnerships and so much more. Avoid the typical and be remembered.

This model also applies when looking for employment opportunities in mental health. Sure, you can send a resume and cover letter to a prospective employer, but a far more effective approach would be to add value to the organization before even applying. Volunteer your time; be part of the solution and earn the right to be heard and recognized. These are two very different approaches.

The take-away from these examples is that new marketing models are incredibly effective. Furthermore, if you're in private practice and looking to thrive, you won't be nearly as effective through traditional marketing approaches. People won't simply come to you just because you make an announcement or two through an advertisement stating you are open for business. It takes more to earn the interest and trust of others. How do you make mental health important and relevant to your market? One way you do so is by becoming part of the conversation people are having both online and offline.

- Offer helpful information.
- Build awareness by sharing your expertise.
- Reach out to others in ways that show you genuinely care about them.

Throughout this book I offer you a wide variety of tools and techniques that will position you in this domain. We begin with a discussion of three unique marketing concepts: Permission Marketing, Sales Progressions, and the use of Traditional Marketing vehicles as part of an overall integrated model.

The Rise of Permission Marketing and Its Use in Mental Health

One of the most important new marketing methods available to you is known as permission marketing. Permission marketing is a term coined by marketing expert Seth Godin. It's a simple but powerful idea, and involves offering people an opportunity to volunteer to receive marketing materials from you. Rather than sending your marketing message out to large groups of people in the hopes of interrupting and gaining their attention, this model seeks to earn the right to engage in an ongoing dialogue with your client base. Let me offer an example to clarify what I mean by this approach.

There is a therapist in Washington, DC who has built a thriving consulting practice using a permission-based model. She offers free training to mental health professionals at least twice a month in the form of lunch-and-learn programs. Her goal with these workshops is not to sign up people for one of her paid programs. Her focus is getting people to commit to the first small step in the selling process. In this case, that process is for attendees to give her their e-mail and/or mailing address so she can send them future updates.

Over the years, she has built an extensive mailing list using this approach. She uses this list to offer even more value by mailing fact sheets and useful resources free of charge. This information reinforces the positive experiences she has already created through her free workshops and leaves a lasting impression. Once again, she uses a permission-based model to continue to build trust and credibility by offering real value to her target market.

The result? Her paid workshops are always in demand. She receives close to a 50% conversion rate when she decides to promote one of her services. In contrast, the industry standard for conversion rates when posting an advertisement in a newspaper or mass mailing a postcard about your practice is 1% to 4% at best.

Her success did not happen instantly; she worked hard at building trust and credibility through her free workshops and worksheets. She built strong relationships in the community that enabled her to create a qualified list of prospects who were interested in what she offered.

And best part of all, her approach is very cost-effective! If you leverage the Internet, it's essentially a *free* direct mail marketing campaign—only better. Why? Because you have already taken a step to qualify your customers, meaning the people who are receiving your marketing material have already expressed interest in you. They want and expect to hear from you!

Sales Progressions: What They Are and Why They Matter

If you look at the Washington, DC therapist scenario a little more closely, you'll notice that she utilizes another important sales and marketing concept known as a Sales Progression. This process is extremely powerful and can have a tremendous positive impact in all areas of your professional life if you understand how to use it appropriately.

A sales progression process consists of a series of steps designed to move someone along a consumer-oriented continuum. The first series of steps typically focuses on building trust. Once trust is earned, a person using this process offers potential customers an opportunity to take some sort of action. The action they take may then be rewarded with a free gift, resources, or some other thing of value. The ultimate goal is to create such a positive experience that the potential customer will take the next step: purchasing a service or product.

Figure 2.4 shows the sales progression process used by the therapist in Washington, DC.

Figure 2.4 *The Sales Progression Process*

The first thing she does is build trust by offering something of value and by demonstrating that she is highly skilled. She doesn't focus on herself, and she doesn't use a hard-sell approach; rather, she chooses to give value to her community in order to build awareness and credibility. Once she earns people's trust they are much more likely to take action. In this case the action she is hoping for is that a person chooses to join her mailing list. She rewards that trust by e-mailing valuable resources and information without making a sales pitch. This, in turn, builds further trust, which also leads the potential customer to begin telling others about the therapist. At this point she now has other people in the community marketing her services through word-of-mouth advertising. Very few sales and marketing techniques are as powerful as word-of-mouth advertising! When the time comes for her to offer a paid seminar, she announces this to her email community, where a high percentage of these people register for the workshop and ask their friends to join them for the experience.

I cannot emphasize enough how effective this process can be for you. You can build sales progressions into your advertisements, your training efforts, and even your job search effort. The uses are only restricted by your imagination.

No matter what you do in the mental health field, I strongly recommend you use sales progressions. I often hear from mental health practitioners who do a great job with the beginning stages of their marketing efforts. They build visibility by doing many of the activities discussed in this chapter (e.g., offering free training sessions, volunteering their time). However, they make the mistake of ending right there. When this happens, their efforts exist in a vacuum. As a result, even if people are positively affected by their efforts there is nothing else for them to do. This is a main reason why people get so frustrated. Their business doesn't grow even after they feel they are using a value-based marketing approach. You must map out a process to target potential prospects so they move along a continuum from curious observer to interested participant to passionate consumer who champions your services in the community.

Don't Discount Traditional Methods Altogether!

There is no doubt that new marketing principles are going to be an important part of business growth and opportunity both now and in the future. However, like everything else, it is not an all-or-nothing proposition. Traditional marketing methods still hold some value for you and should not be discounted altogether.

In my organization I continue to use television and print ads to deliver a message to potential clients. However, when doing so, I am mindful of the strengths and weaknesses of these media, and because I know this, I am much smarter about the way I choose to use these vehicles. I use a combination of traditional and new marketing methods that best address the unique needs of my business.

Let me offer a more specific example.

When my behavioral healthcare organization chooses to reach a large audience through traditional marketing channels, we make sure to pay particular attention to how we will best leverage this effort and how we can quickly shift to a newer marketing model. When we develop a print advertisement for a local publication, we know that on some level this advertisement is intended to gain attention by "interrupting" the reader. We design the advertisement to have clarity of purpose, whereby the reader is compelled to take some sort of action that might lead to use of our services.

It's here that we make the shift to a newer marketing model. We don't necessarily expect the print ad to lead to direct use of our inpatient services; rather, our focus with the ad is twofold. We want the reader to either call our assessment line for a free consultation or go to our web site, where they can sign up to be on our online mailing list.

If they choose to call us, we look to build a strong relationship by offering a tremendous customer service experience. Our intent is for the caller to receive help regardless of whether they need inpatient treatment services at that time. We build trust by offering help in any way possible because we are thinking long-term with our marketing efforts. The customer service experience becomes our new marketing vehicle.

If, on the other hand, they choose to go to our web site, we make certain to offer the reader valuable information on the site in the hope that they will give us permission to e-mail future announcements, newsletters, and resources to them. Our online presence is designed to foster a community of people who are interested in mental health. In essence, we gain influence through the development of a large database of e-mail addresses from people who signed up to receive future updates. This gives us the option to launch a free online mailer campaign. These campaigns are not only cost-effective; they are also far more powerful for the simple reason that we are marketing to people who want and expect to hear from us. Our e-mail campaigns are anticipated, more targeted, and read at a much higher percentage than a more traditional mailer campaign. This is the power of a new marketing approach.

This is one example of many, and I would encourage you to think about your business needs and tailor a marketing program to best meet those needs. If you're a solo practitioner, for instance, you may choose to forgo all traditional marketing options until you are more established. Your best approach might be to identify a long-term permission-based marketing model that will give you an opportunity to build credibility and visibility in the community with more impact and less cost than if you chose to advertise on the radio or in a local magazine.

My point here is to emphasize that new marketing vehicles are available to you and give you a tremendous amount of flexibility. In addition, they speak to the new needs and desires of clients who have too many choices and not enough time. People can easily ignore what you have to say unless it speaks directly to them. This is where a new approach to marketing can have a big impact for you!

WHERE CAN MARKETING TAKE YOU?

Over the years, I've learned many things about marketing and selling professional mental health services. And as you have seen in this chapter, there is much more to marketing than meets the eye. So what have we learned thus far?

If you understand the strengths and weaknesses of traditional marketing models, you'll begin to use these forms of advertising in much smarter ways. You've already seen how my behavioral health care organization learned to use traditional marketing channels within the context of a greater system. Like this organization, you have the ability to create a more diverse and sophisticated marketing approach that reaches out and speaks to the unique needs of your audience. In addition, you now have a greater understanding and appreciation of newer forms of marketing. You have the ability to use permission marketing and sales progressions in a fashion similar to the Washington, DC therapist who uses these techniques so effectively. In this realm you can give people the opportunity to benefit from your unique skills by becoming an integral part of their communities. You also have the opportunity to reach out to others on a much grander scale by embracing technology and engaging people in real conversations that matter. *The ClueTrain Manifesto* predicted this market shift years ago, and it serves as a reminder of what it takes to gain the attention of people in your community and beyond.

People are searching and waiting for someone who speaks to them. They are looking for fresh ideas and exciting opportunities for personal growth. All they need is a chance to access them. You can introduce them to those opportunities through your marketing efforts.

There is much more for us to learn and we will continue our exploration in subsequent chapters. But as a starting point, know this—the marketing techniques I propose are not based on calculated messages and manipulation. They are not about competing and winning. One of the most exciting things about what I am proposing with this marketing model is that you can achieve the success you desire by following your passion, living your ideals, and sharing them with others. And it is this approach, now more than ever, that is having the greatest impact in the marketplace.

SUMMARY

- Selling is the act of persuading or influencing a client to buy a product or service, while marketing is everything you do to reach clients and to build awareness. Marketing is the message that prepares the prospect for a sale.
- In today's marketplace, effective marketing involves much more than the traditional advertising campaigns we are all accustomed to. New marketing is about connecting people, creating excitement, and building trust. It is about building relationships, solving problems for people, and offering value that cannot be ignored.
- Traditional Marketing is losing its power for two main reasons: (1) People are simply overloaded with information. As a result, they must choose what messages to let in and what messages to ignore. (2) In addition, the marketplace today is incredibly diverse and offers consumers more choices than ever before. People with choices do not need to compromise. They will not settle for something that is good when they see something else that is outstanding.
- Permission Marketing concerns itself with earning permission to market to people. Rather than send your messages out to the masses, you take steps to position your service and/or product in a way that allows you to focus on those who want to hear from you.
- A sales progression consists of a series of steps designed to move a potential customer from one step to another. An example would be hearing about your business and taking the step of looking at your web site. If you do a good job of offering value to the Web reader then that person might take another step and become a registered member of the site.

And receiving additional value might result in taking the next step, which is calling you to schedule an appointment.

- Using a new marketing model will help distinguish you in the market-place. People are looking for businesses and professionals who understand their needs and listen to what they have to say. Those who do not take this approach are the ones who are largely ignored.

CHAPTER THREE

How to Sell Mental Health Services

Five Elements of Success

A New Sales Philosophy for Mental Health Professionals

We've taken a closer look at important marketing concepts and discussed their application within the mental health profession. Now let's take a closer look at the next piece of the puzzle — sales skills and the art of selling mental health services. As you will soon see, a sophisticated sales approach offers behavioral health care practitioners a wealth of opportunity.

One of the golden nuggets within the sales profession is the understanding that the most powerful sales skills, principles, and models are those that contribute to a fundamental shift in how business is conducted.

What is this shift? The shift I am referring to is a movement away from participating in the selling process to becoming an important and critical part of the buying process. Sales experts across the globe emphasize the importance of this paradigm shift in order to achieve high levels of success.

What does it mean when you talk about moving from the selling process to the buying process? Simply put, the selling process, in and of itself, can be a difficult and unrewarding endeavor. At its core it is a process whereby you are not in a position of strength, where you tend to focus on your own interests, and where you must seek out and convince others to use your services.

Now, what would life be like as a practitioner if others sought you versus you seeking them? What if people recognized you as an authority in the field who could help with their needs? What would it be like if the people you came in contact with were already willing buyers? When a change occurs where you are highly visible within the marketplace and where you are viewed as a valuable resource and partner, people begin to seek you out without any soliciting on your part. Business comes to you, and you inevitably reach those who are ready to buy versus soliciting those who have little to no interest. Your business approach attracts people who want to buy versus spending time trying to convince people to buy!

A Mental Health Example

Let's say you're a mental health clinician who has been in the field many years, have expertise in family/child issues, and decide to offer a group on parenting skills. You attend networking events, but find that everyone at those events is pitching their own service and not seeking services to buy. Attendees shower you with praise and tout your service as "much needed" and "long overdue." However, you generate little to no business from those events. You advertise your group to doctors' offices and through basic networking channels such as local counseling chapters and school systems. Still no one comes.

The issue here is not necessarily missing the mark in terms of community needs and it is not an issue of skill and competence. A main reason why you are unable to fill the seats is because you have not tapped into the buying process. In the buying scenario, you would have built a level of credibility in the community, you would have communicated value, built awareness, and positioned yourself in such a way that people had to go through you in order to access these specific mental health services. Your sales approach and philosophy would prompt those in the community to recognize you, talk about you, and value you as an important resource.

In addition, you would have created highly effective communication channels and systems and offered solutions that removed traditional barriers or obstacles to buying. This last component is perhaps most critical of all to business success, since these systems encourage and allow others to take the next step toward utilizing your services. If you can create this shift your ability to grow as a practitioner multiplies exponentially and with half of the effort.

I have grouped many best practice sales skills and approaches into Core Sales Principles to help clarify and organize these concepts in a way that makes sense. They are extremely powerful principles in that they all contribute to the fundamental shift that repositions the practitioner from selling to buying. Taken as a whole, they offer readers a comprehensive and effective foundation that top performing businesses and sales professionals use to reach the pinnacle of success within their industry.

Let's take a closer look at each of these principles.

CREATING A BUYING ENVIRONMENT THROUGH CLIENT-BASED SELLING

Many people in all areas of business mistakenly take an approach that sells their services rather than their solutions. A distinguishing factor for most people who are successful within their industry is that they are customer-focused, meaning they sell the way the customer wants to buy. These people focus solely on the needs, problems, and wants of the customer and work to find solutions that will help that customer. This concept sounds basic and simple, but it takes dedication and a high level of skill to be client-focused in the area of selling. Let's take a look at some of the key elements associated with a customer-based approach so you may see how to effectively incorporate this principle within the scope of your practice.

Element 1: Sell the Way People Want to Buy

> "You can make more friends in two months by becoming interested in other people, than you can in two years by trying to get other people interested in you."
>
> —*Dale Carnegie (1981, p. 54)*

This quote, from Dale Carnegie, offers a glimpse into one of the most critical aspects of effective selling. It provides the reader with a key link between human behavior and the law of attraction that will bring about positive sales results for you. Focus on others, and you will generate far more powerful results!

Turning On the Lights

In my work I meet with many mental health practitioners throughout the day to talk about and sell behavioral health services. In the beginning, my approach consisted of arriving at a scheduled sales appointment and quickly launching into a discussion about all the services our psychiatric hospital had to offer. Since I was a clinician by training, I felt I knew what my prospects were looking for, and so I spent a lot of time talking about the specifics of our clinical product. I thought this approach would help distinguish me in the marketplace, and therefore, benefit the bottom line of my employer.

My belief in the approach I was using, however, began to change several months into my new role. During that time, I met with a psychiatrist who worked for a local hospital in our area. As usual, I quickly launched into my talk about services because I felt he was quite busy and did not have much time to give. I discussed many different things and handed him various materials that he brushed aside. I continued discussing the details of our services until he interrupted me with two questions: "Do you use a traditional substance abuse treatment model within your detox program? One that adheres strictly to the 12-step traditions?" The questions seemed to come from left field, as I had not even discussed our substance abuse programs at that point. I could have easily responded to his question. However, for some reason on this day I paused and said, "That's a good question. Why do you ask?" I assumed his answer would be either that he was a strong believer in the model or he was not. Instead, he informed me he had a patient who needed detox services and most likely longer-term treatment for alcohol addiction. The patient was also on psychotropic meds and painkillers for severe chronic back pain. He went on to tell me he often works with complex cases like this, but he does not know where to send them since many treatment facilities are not sympathetic to these situations; and they will not provide substance abuse treatment services unless the patients are off all medications.

Wow! This was valuable information, and I would not have obtained it if he had not interrupted my speech about child services and if I had simply answered his first question. Luckily, my response helped uncover the true meaning behind his question, and this gave me an opportunity to answer him more effectively and offer real solutions based on his specific needs. I was able to tell him that our organization did work with cases such as the one he mentioned and that our physicians and clinical team were comfortable working with an approach that allowed other medications that were helping with existing medical conditions. I also provided him with the names of the psychiatrists to contact should he have further questions about the overall clinical approach.

That meeting was a revelation for me. I made a positive impression during the sales call that to this day has led to many substance abuse treatment referrals from that particular psychiatrist. As a result, I decided to take this approach more often. Instead of talking incessantly about our services, I structured my meetings to focus on the needs of the customer first and foremost. I began taking more time to prepare beforehand so I could ask targeted questions based on my audience's area of expertise and services. I spoke less and listened more to what they had to say. Ultimately, I discovered that this approach helped me understand the true hot buttons and needs of the client versus simply giving them a generic overview of our services. As a result, I was able to gear my talk specifically to those needs. This inevitably led to the development of a much stronger emotional connection that was further amplified when I was also able to offer solutions to their needs and problems. This process alone served to create a positive impression for our organization that led to improved relationships and increased sales. In addition, this client-focused approach inevitably encouraged an open dialogue with those organizations that were not using our services, and in many instances I was able to clear up misunderstandings or remove barriers so that our organization became a useful resource for their practice.

And How *Does This Pertain to Me?*

You may be asking yourself, what in the world does this example about selling mental health services have to do with me and the clinical work I am doing?! How does this approach, this philosophy, possibly fit into my world? My short answer is this—it does fit, and it can do a lot for you!!

For starters, use this model to better understand your client's needs so that you can create a buying environment for your client base. If you're an organization, a customer-focused approach helps you understand the marketplace so you can position yourself more effectively. If you are a practitioner within a larger organization and you use this approach with colleagues and clients, you will better understand the needs and expectations of your organization, you will build stronger professional relationships, and you will position yourself for growth and promotional opportunities within the company. If you're an individual practitioner, you will offer services that speak to the needs of the client, you'll stand out from the crowd as someone who listens and understands their needs. I encourage you to get out and meet people in your community. Create opportunities for dialogue and ask good questions; learn people's problems, needs, and challenges. Use this information to identify and develop unique solutions. You'll be remembered for your efforts, and people will begin seeking you out.

Element 2: *The Power of Presence: Listen First, Talk Last, and Ask Excellent Questions*

It is the rare individual who truly focuses on the customer in the here and now. In today's world people lose sight of this fact and steer themselves toward meeting their own specific needs. It's certainly not hard to do! With work demands, family responsibilities, and personal and professional financial worries, it is no wonder that we lose sight of others and focus within. Sales departments are notorious in this regard as they often institute aggressive quotas and systems that encourage sales professionals to neglect their clients and instead focus on their own demands and requirements. As a result, a practical, long-term, and customer-oriented approach becomes a rarity in any industry.

Shifting one's focus to the customer starts with being fully present and listening to others. Does this sound familiar? If you are a mental health practitioner, it should sound all too familiar. Sophisticated and powerful sales skills adopt skill sets that are very similar to core clinical skills all mental health professionals are trained to use. Empathy, Active Listening, Being Present for the Client, Asking Open Ended Questions, Reflecting Feeling and Content, and Problem Solving are just a few of the clinical techniques you can use to become outstanding at meeting client needs and selling your services.

Feature-Oriented versus Solution-Oriented Selling

In **feature-oriented selling** the focus is on the person selling the service. He or she launches into a detailed discussion about what they do and what they offer right from the beginning. This is the approach I used previously. I would arrive at a meeting and monopolize the conversation by bombarding the prospect with facts and features about all our services. When I was not talking, the internal dialogue in my head made it virtually impossible to take in what my client was really saying. This model is the most common one you'll find, in spite of the fact that it is a self-serving and clumsy approach that rarely gets at the specific needs of the prospect.

I am not saying that features and details about your service or product are unimportant. Your ability to offer high-quality services is an essential part of the selling process. What I am saying here is that you must uncover the needs of the customer and *then* determine how your services can best meet those needs.

A **solution-focused approach** shifts the spotlight from you, the seller, to the potential client. Rather than talking about features you offer, you take time to understand the unique needs of clients and then identify solutions based on their needs. How do you do this? You accomplish this by asking good questions, giving people an opportunity to share their story, and then probing to uncover needs. Once you have achieved this, you provide the customer with solutions that are specific to his or her unique needs. The results of making this shift are tremendous and a change in process will benefit you in ways beyond simply selling a service or product.

One clinician I met had tremendous success using this approach, and she would take this concept well beyond what I am describing in this section. She often spoke at community luncheons and school functions as a way to give back to the community, to keep in tune with the needs and challenges of the community, and to ultimately sell herself. After a lengthy dialogue about needs of specific families, she would determine whether she could help them. If she determined it was outside her scope, she used her network in the community to offer solutions that did not involve her. She would refer people to other professionals she believed would be a better fit. She went even beyond this! Rather than offering contact information, she would go through the effort of setting up an appointment for that person and would follow up to ensure everything worked out. I asked her why she went to all the trouble, and she informed me that the simple act of helping others, even if it did not directly help her, actually had the long-term effect of benefiting her. She reported that this was perhaps her single most effective and rewarding sales approach, and it gave her an excellent reputation both in the community and with her colleagues, who returned the favor by sending referrals her way. It had a tremendous snowball effect.

What Is a Good Sales Question?

Good questions are as important in sales as they are in clinical work. In the sales profession those who ask good, targeted questions at appropriate times are those who uncover the buying needs of potential clients. It is very enticing to quickly answer a question when you feel you have an easy answer. However, in most cases, patience is the key to unlocking a treasure chest of opportunity. Here are six samples of good questions often used by sales professionals during the sales process. These questions are very useful in ensuring the focus is on the client and in uncovering important information about a potential client's needs and wants. Use these as a framework and try to come up with your own questions to help you identify client needs.

1. "That's an interesting question. Why do you ask?"
   - This is an excellent clarifying question that will limit quick judgments and assumptions.
   - Use this question as an alternative to answering their initial question. This is very effective when someone asks about your specific services and/or programs.
2. "When you ask about treatment programs for anxiety, what is it specifically that you are looking for?"
   - Once again, this is a good clarifying question, and will help you get more targeted answers.
3. End with a question after responding to someone else's question.
   - "Is this accurate?" "Does that make sense?"
4. "What's been your experience with. . . ."
   - This will give you an idea as to what someone might like or dislike about a particular service.
5. "When I say 'parenting treatment program,' what one word comes to mind?"
   - The answer to this question will give you top-of-mind awareness and access to an individual's needs, biases, and feelings associated with that topic.
   - Once a word has been provided, it is also effective to ask a follow-up question that leads to a more detailed discussion. "Okay, so 'sympathy' was the first thing that came to mind. Tell me more about the reason(s) why you chose that word."

6. Silence is golden.

- Once you ask a question, make an effort to remain silent and give the person an opportunity to think and respond.
- Interrupting too quickly may interfere with the flow of the conversation and serve to derail you in your efforts to uncover need.

Element 3: Give Value and Business Will Follow!

The importance of value in business is painfully obvious to most. However, what may not be so obvious is the concept of "value" that I am referring to here. The term *value* as defined in this new approach to selling is different than the more traditional model where value and benefit is the direct result of professional services and/or products that are purchased. My definition of value within this new sales model is:

Delivering something to potential clients without any expectation of something in return.

This approach proposes finding opportunities to give value to people that goes beyond a typical fee for service model. It is a completely altruistic and giving concept.

Take a look at these two questions about marketing approaches and ask yourself which one is more powerful.

- Do potential clients and/or referral sources want another brochure or announcement about a service you are delivering?
- Would they be more interested in a referral you provide to their practice, a resource that can help grow their business, or a free educational program offering helpful tips that will make their lives better?

Offering value as identified in the second bullet point is a powerful sales and marketing tool! Clients and referral sources *always* have time for valuable information that will help them personally or professionally. Using this model will open doors that are otherwise closed and will give you the opportunity to reach others on a different level.

One exercise I find extremely useful for my own work is the practice of identifying a list of resources and services I can give potential clients that are *high on value*. I try to do this periodically to keep myself focused on long-term growth. Some examples you'll find on my list are:

- Creating a web site offering updated resource information
- Offering a blog with a weekly post on sales and marketing concepts
- Creating a sorted resource directory for practitioners
- Offering to promote other people's services and programs

- Providing free educational opportunities for professional development
- Finding employment opportunities for others
- Referring business to clinicians

The Power of Value: A Mental Health Example

As I mentioned previously, my job is to sell services for a large behavioral healthcare organization. One day I held a lunch meeting at a local practice consisting of a team of psychiatrists and psychotherapists. I knew most of the professionals within the practice—all except one psychiatrist whom I had never been able to meet. Sales representatives of all kinds constantly solicited her, and as a result, she made a decision to restrict sales calls. None of my efforts to meet her had worked in the past, and this day was no exception. During our lunch meeting, she dropped in unexpectedly, grabbed a sandwich, and then said, "David, a friend of mine is moving to the Charleston area. She is a psychiatrist and is looking for employment opportunities. Do you know if your organization has any opportunities?"

I told her I would look into the matter and asked for her friend's name and contact information. She provided me with the information, thanked me, and left the room.

I knew we probably did not have any job opportunities at that point in time, but I also knew this was a very good opportunity to make a positive impression. I decided I would put together a plan to help this psychiatrist in any way I could, whether with our organization or another provider. I called the psychiatrist and told her I wanted to help her get connected with my organization, and we set up an appointment to meet face-to-face when she was in town. Prior to the meeting, I researched practices that in the past had mentioned to me they were looking for a psychiatrist. I also developed a list of questions to learn more about her, her interests, and her area of expertise.

After our meeting, I contacted my medical director and had him call the new psychiatrist to set up a face-to-face meeting. I also called two of the larger practices in the area who had casually mentioned to me that they were looking for additional psychiatrists. I had both practices call her to schedule interviews. One week following our meeting she had three interviews scheduled. She interviewed at all three places but did not take a job with any of the leads I provided. Instead, she chose to join a different organization in the community.

I recall hearing from our medical director after the entire process. He said that during their meeting she mentioned not knowing why I was going through all this trouble to help her. The answer is easy—The Power of Value!

When people hear this story, many say that I went through all that trouble and she didn't even join one of the practices I provided. As a result, they viewed it as wasted time. The reality and the irony is that the most effective sales interventions are often those that are not directly involved in selling. Another reality is recognizing that everyone is a potential customer, and every interaction is a selling moment. Let's take a look at the outcomes resulting from my efforts and see how giving value benefited my organization.

What were the outcomes of this event for my organization and me?

- *Instant credibility* with a psychiatrist who had refused to see me in the past. She now sees my company as a valuable resource. **Next time I call on her, will I get an appointment? Might she consider our organization if she has a service need?**
- *A new prospect in our market* now views my organization as a valuable resource and partner. **Will she refer to my company? Will she talk with colleagues about her experience?**
- *Strengthening existing relationships.* Two of my top accounts were grateful I thought of them. They contact our organization whenever they have a question about behavioral healthcare needs, and this has led to increased referrals.
- *Talk in the community.* The best kind of marketing comes when other people talk about you. The chances are good that this new psychiatrist talked to others about the help she received.
- *Becoming part of the buying process.* Instead of me chasing business, business is now chasing me. I have tapped into the buying process!

My hope is that you can see how this kind of value-based approach can help you and your practice. The model can be used in numerous areas within mental health. Whether you are searching for a new job opportunity, in private practice, or working for an organization, this approach will build relationships, identify referral channels, and help grow your business.

Element 4: Arouse "Want" and "Need" in Others

The most profound teachers stand the test of time and Dale Carnegie is no exception. In 1912 he began teaching classes on human behavior and the power of persuasion and in 1936 wrote his now-renowned book, *How to Win Friends and Influence People.* Today it continues to hold significant weight in the world of business—particularly in professional sales.

One of the more interesting insights found in his book is: "The only way on earth to influence other people is to talk about what they want and show them how to get it." He goes on: "Of course you are interested in what you want.

You are eternally interested in it. But no one else is. The rest of us are just like you: we are interested in what we want."

Mr. Carnegie speaks of a fundamental concept I attempt to emphasize throughout this book: Your ability to influence people is directly proportional to your willingness to understand the needs and wants of others!

Want to learn how to attract business and succeed in this field and beyond?

Arouse in the other person a desire and need by focusing on their desires and solving their problems, thereby creating an environment where a person will want to buy.

Do You Really Know What Your Clients Are Looking For?

We've already discussed the importance of good questioning to identify client needs. Another way to better understand your target audience is through the use of brainstorming exercises.

One such exercise is a free association activity that can be done alone or in a group setting. It is an excellent activity for those looking to identify key messages that speak directly to customer need. It involves a simple four-step process, as shown in Table 3.1.

Table 3.1 *Free Association Exercise*

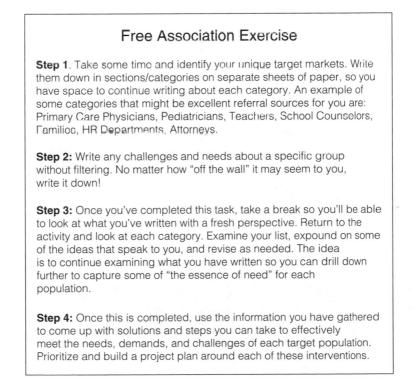

Free Association Exercise

Step 1: Take some time and identify your unique target markets. Write them down in sections/categories on separate sheets of paper, so you have space to continue writing about each category. An example of some categories that might be excellent referral sources for you are: Primary Care Physicians, Pediatricians, Teachers, School Counselors, Families, HR Departments, Attorneys.

Step 2: Write any challenges and needs about a specific group without filtering. No matter how "off the wall" it may seem to you, write it down!

Step 3: Once you've completed this task, take a break so you'll be able to look at what you've written with a fresh perspective. Return to the activity and look at each category. Examine your list, expound on some of the ideas that speak to you, and revise as needed. The idea is to continue examining what you have written so you can drill down further to capture some of "the essence of need" for each population.

Step 4: Once this is completed, use the information you have gathered to come up with solutions and steps you can take to effectively meet the needs, demands, and challenges of each target population. Prioritize and build a project plan around each of these interventions.

Here are some examples of what the outcomes from Steps 1 through 3 might look like.

Primary Care Physicians

- Very busy work environment. A lot of patients seen in a short time frame.
- Tend to not want to take time to meet with you to discuss their needs.
- They want easy access to services. Speed is key!
- They want to know the services are reliable and of high quality so they do not have to take time following up.
- You get one shot to make an impression. If it works, they will continue using you.
- Their end goal: to keep mental health issues away from their office so they can focus on areas they are most comfortable with.

Teachers

- They have high stress jobs and are asked to manage many things (students, school demands/requirements, parents).
- Key stressors: behavioral problems in the classroom, unmanageable and/or threatening children, parents who are uneducated as to psychological and developmental problems.
- They want education and practical tools and processes showing them how to identify problem areas and how to address situations effectively.
- They want knowledge and awareness of psychological and developmental issues that will make them more effective in the classroom.
- They want a relationship and partnership with a professional they trust, someone to help them so they can refer families and children quickly and with peace of mind knowing they are getting the care and support they need.
- They need good mental health resources so they can focus on other demands of their job such as standardized testing.

Families

- They want someone who can help their child quickly.
- They want someone who understands their needs and anxieties.
- They want someone who is an expert in their field.
- They want someone who is referred to them by another.
- They want someone who is visible and known in the community.

- Their challenges might be denial and a general unwillingness to seek treatment for themselves or their child.

Hiring Manager

- A hiring manager who is posting a position has a specific need. If she has an open position, this may be impacting her ability to be an effective manager, it may be impacting the quality of services, and it may be having a negative impact on her team.
- This manager may be doing two jobs until she fills the other position. For example, she may be managing a team and taking a caseload in order to meet the overall service needs. She may be putting other important projects on hold until she can find additional resources.
- She is looking to fill the position quickly.
- She is looking for someone who is reliable and committed so she does not have to worry about filling the position again.
- She wants someone who will be easy to manage, meaning the person gets along well with others, can function in a changing, fast paced environment, can work independently, and be counted on to complete tasks.
- She wants someone who is skilled clinically and/or can learn quickly.
- She wants someone who has initiative and the drive to learn new concepts and incorporate those into new service offerings.

These are merely examples of what the initial brainstorming steps might look like. The process in and of itself will help you better understand customer needs so that you can provide services that reach out to your target audience in ways that will lead to success.

Here are some examples of what solutions you might come up with in Step 4. (Note that these are actual examples provided by clinicians.)

Primary Care Physicians

- Offer a streamlined referral process making it easy for patients to schedule an appointment (e.g., online appointment scheduler, VIP status for a specific medical practice).
- Offer a "day at the office" service where you work out an arrangement to see walk-in clients and/or address patient issues with physicians during a set day/time.
- Obtain endorsements from physicians in the community to share with other physicians as part of a marketing campaign. Stress expertise, reliability, and speed/ease of service access.

- Provide medical practice doctors and staff with a detailed mental health resource list to include practitioners by specialty area, treatment groups, support groups, and other community programs.

Teachers

- Participate in specific school initiatives at both a local and county level to help solve a mental health issue (e.g., offer assistance in setting up an appropriate assessment and emergency response process for children who become aggressive and/or out of control at school).
- Offer free educational workshops for teachers, complete with practical tips to help with classroom management and basic assessment skills so teachers know when to refer out quickly.
- Build relationships and partnerships with guidance counseling departments and offer services and systems to make their jobs easier and more effective.

The Power of Persuasion and Influence

Think back and remember a time when you were persuaded to do something. A time when you felt good about your decision to take action, and the outcome was a positive one for you. Can you remember how this process went for you and how the persuasive person approached you? Can you compare that to a time when you may have been pressured into making a decision and regretted it? Often the best way to learn how the power of persuasion works is to reflect on your own experiences. When you review some of these episodes, try to remember the key elements present during those positive experiences. Think about how you can incorporate some of these elements into your own process of reaching out to potential consumers. That is where the gold is!

In short, persuasion is a partnership process where you work together to solve problems and come up with mutually beneficial solutions. It is manipulation-free, which also means it is long-term in focus and is designed to create a win-win situation.

The reality is that people do not like to be sold to, and as a result, aggressive self-serving sales tactics turn people away. These tactics are short-term focused due to the fact that the experience is often a negative one for the consumer. However, we all have needs and problems that need solutions. If someone approaches us with a product or service that will address our needs, then a buying environment is created and we are compelled to buy.

What Manipulation Looks Like

One of the reasons mental health practitioners cringe when they hear about the idea of selling is the impression they have of pushy sales professionals using manipulative tactics. In the past, and still somewhat today, sales experts teach specific techniques and interventions that are designed to manipulate another person into buying. This often involves use of slick sales lines and high-pressure sales tactics, whereby the salesperson believes that somehow and some way they can trick a potential customer into buying.

Let's have a little fun and take a look at some closing techniques that are still alive and well within the old school sales mentality. You may have been the victim of these in the past.

The Save Face Close

- This approach involves shaming potential consumers in the hope that they feel pressured into buying.
- An example might be, "I certainly understand, as not everyone is really ready for this kind of advanced training."
- Another example: "Well, I hear you. We are a top-of-the-line producer, so this product is not something everyone can afford."

The Build Up Close

- A salesperson uses this technique by asking a series of questions to which the answer is undoubtedly yes.
- The theory behind this is to get potential customers to agree with you so that they'll say yes when the time comes to ask for the sale.

It will come as no surprise to you to know that these techniques rarely work, and they are virtual killers when looking at long-term business success and growth.

So while others may choose to aggressively pursue and pressure potential customers into buying, you can differentiate yourself and widen the gap between you and your competition by identifying ways to *give people what they want*.

Element 5: Go Above and Beyond and Be Remembered!

When I was living in Washington, DC following graduate school, I had the good fortune of meeting an experienced and talented clinician who took me under her wing. I was amazed at how well her practice grew and prospered. While other clinicians struggled to survive, she was opening satellite offices in Maryland and Northern Virginia. While other practitioners complained about poor pay and limited opportunities, she was looking to hire new clinicians to support the constant flow of business coming her way.

She had many skills and did many things that led to her success, but for me the number one reason for her success was the fact that *she always made a powerful impression, and she always stood out from the crowd.*

No matter where you were in the DC Metro area, if you mentioned her name, people knew her in a positive light. Most knew her because they had benefited directly from something she had offered them.

One example I recall was a conversation about childhood trauma between several DSS and DMH workers. During the conversation her name was mentioned. The group spoke about an experience they had with her one year before when DSS called and asked her for some suggestions about books and papers on childhood trauma. Instead of simply offering references she proposed meeting to discuss other things that might help achieve their goal. She proposed offering an eight-session parenting program, which contained principles of childhood trauma as one component. She offered to deliver the workshop once a week on the weekends. She came up with a detailed program, found space through her connections, solicited involvement from other experts in the area, and put together a top-notch training program. Before you knew it, DSS was putting on a comprehensive workshop for community members that received a lot of positive attention in Washington, DC. Best of all—she did all this for *free*!

I learned a great deal from her over the years, but perhaps the greatest lesson was to approach my work and my profession in a way that would be memorable, helpful to others, and unique. Becoming memorable essentially means adopting characteristics and principles that will distinguish you in the marketplace. Since then I have continued to identify areas and factors I believe contribute to the goal of creating a positive impression and being remembered. The pages that follow identify a few of these important factors.

Be Giving

In my mind, the power of giving has no equal. Sharing your expertise and giving value to others will expand your network and presence in the field at an incredible rate.

Building trust begins a sales progression process whereby potential clients, referral sources, and business partners learn to trust and respect what you have to say. Once you've earned their confidence, you present them with options to take action, and if they choose to act, you offer additional value and assistance. This repeated and genuine process of giving will more than likely be rewarded (e.g., a referral, signing up for initial session, registration for a seminar, word-of-mouth advertising).

And how do you earn someone's trust? You accomplish this by thinking of ways to help individuals, community organizations, and the like. There are all kinds of ways to network and to market yourself, however, most of these efforts are meaningless and ineffective if you don't offer genuine value. Many marketing efforts and tools fall on deaf ears not because they aren't useful, but because they're not linked to a process that's focused on offering value and building trust.

Here are some examples that are lacking in the value department.

- Showing up at "power" networking events and giving out your card to lots of people
- Mass mailing your brochure
- Dropping in to say hello to potential referral resources
- Tracking how many business friends you have on social networking web sites like LinkedIn and Facebook

The networking that matters most of all is the kind that helps people in some way, shape, or form. At its core it involves helping people achieve their goals.

But the act of giving is not enough. It must truly come from the heart. It must be genuine.

I am relentless in this regard. Some would say obsessed! If someone is struggling with an issue or has a specific need, I will do whatever I can to help them even if it's not directly within the scope of my work. This benefits me in two ways.

- First, I simply enjoy helping others.
- Second, it makes me memorable.

If you need a resource, I'll do the research and find what you need. If you're in private practice and looking to expand your referral base, I'll introduce you to some practices that will help generate business. If you're a new counselor who has just gotten out of graduate school, I'll spend time trying to help you break into the field.

You can make similar efforts. A family might be in need of after-school support for their child, and you might know the perfect program or clinician. Or maybe you have a new area of expertise you'd like to share by offering a free seminar. You might even find time to help out a struggling state resource by volunteering your time and expertise.

And while you are doing so always remember: Giving gives back! (See Figure 3.1.)

Final Thought #1:
Giving Gives Back!

Figure 3.1 The Power of Giving

Give Others the Credit

My friend and mentor in Washington, DC was a master at using this principle. Notice that I said DSS received a lot of positive attention in the community for the childhood trauma program. At first I remember thinking that DSS did nothing but follow my mentor's lead. She did all the work! My mentor quickly reminded me that they provided the spark, the funding, and generated enough publicity to make it a success. So in the end, she made sure that DSS received ultimate ownership and the lion's share of praise. The rewards to her would come later on and would be far more powerful.

Behavioral Science researchers talk about an all-important law of human conduct, and years ago Dale Carnegie stated the law in these terms:

"Make the other person feel important—and do it sincerely." (1981, p. 111)

The last piece of this statement is very important since I do not mean to propose giving praise when it is not warranted. But take time to recognize the contributions of others, put your ego aside, and ensure they receive their due. Acknowledging others and appreciating their efforts will help you whether you are a manager, employee, executive, or private practitioner. The process will create a memorable experience for all involved (see Figure 3.2).

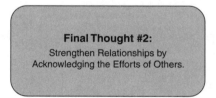

Final Thought #2:
Strengthen Relationships by
Acknowledging the Efforts of Others.

Figure 3.2 Acknowledge the Efforts of Others

Be Better Prepared

Have you ever had a moment during a talk or a meeting when you were prepared to shut off all systems and drift away into daydream land only to find yourself re-energized and completely involved because of what someone had to say? In my experience, these moments are few and far between. However, when they happen they leave a lasting impression. Usually, these moments occur because someone has identified a key area of interest for you, and the ability to achieve this is the direct result of their preparation and, ultimately, understanding of needs and wants.

Yes, this is common sense to a degree. Yet who among us can say we are truly prepared in a way that will impress and engage? I mentioned previously that during my sales calls I came to realize that I needed to shift my focus to the customer. Before my meetings I would research the business, recall my notes on past conversations, and review current market shifts; then I would prepare a series of questions I was prepared to ask during the meeting. In short—I was much better prepared than I had been in the past. It made me sharper and helped me to better engage the person I was speaking with, because I knew what they were doing, understood their demands, and was offering solutions specific to their needs.

In the sales world, I have seen people impress prospects with their knowledge of the person's business. Their efforts quickly engaged the prospect, and they were immediately viewed as someone who could truly help.

As a clinician, you can adopt this approach and use it in similar fashion. One great way to accomplish this is to create opportunities where you meet directly with potential clients and ask them questions that get at need and buyer motivation. Many clinicians feel they have great services to offer in the form of workshops and groups. However, when they offer and market the service, they struggle to create demand. I suggest taking more of a market research approach. When you have a speaking engagement or when you are doing work out in the community, take time to hear what people have to say, and see if you notice important patterns. This will provide you with valuable information so you are much better prepared to speak the client's language and to craft service offerings that are in direct alignment with their underlying needs (see Figure 3.3).

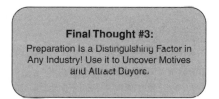

Figure 3.3 The Importance of Preparation

Over-Deliver and Follow Through

Not too long ago, a physician approached our CEO to let her know how thankful he was for all the help he received from the person who represented her organization. He said,

"You know, people always say they will do something, but in reality they make empty promises. This woman actually followed through on what she said she would do and went well beyond my wildest expectations. In my experience, no one ever does that."

It's true—people rarely follow through and almost never exceed expectations. A great way to create an impression is to find ways to help others and to follow through 100% of the time. Be fanatical about it! It will build a strong networking system for you, and it is a great way to create word-of-mouth advertising. Be known as a person who delivers in a big, big way.

Also know that this concept applies to all areas large and small. I once worked with someone who rarely, if ever, returned phone calls. Yes, she was extremely busy and overwhelmed at times; however, this left a negative impression with people. Try your best not to leave things unfinished. Lack of follow-through, however small, is a powerful psychological phenomenon, and it can be a sales killer.

The bottom line is to always think follow-through. Give it a try. It will benefit you no matter what your work setting, and it will create a positive impression with colleagues, supervisors, clients, and prospects alike (see Figure 3.4).

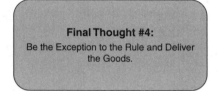

Final Thought #4:
Be the Exception to the Rule and Deliver
the Goods.

Figure 3.4   Follow Through

Everyone Is a Client, and Every Situation Is a Selling Opportunity
I was once asked why in the world I was always helping people find job opportunities and why I was providing workshops and training for graduate students. "You aren't in human resources, and you aren't a teacher. It's not your job."

On the contrary! It is most definitely my job! In reality, everyone is a potential client in one way, shape, or form and the same principle applies to you.

I enjoy helping others find new employment opportunities in the field. And down the road, when they are in that job and they have a client who needs intensive treatment services, my hope is that they will think of me and give a call. When I deliver trainings to graduate students and help them find internships, I recall those days when I needed help getting started in the field. I enjoy sharing my lessons learned in the hope that my efforts will prevent them from making similar mistakes! But my motives aren't entirely altruistic. Delivering trainings in the community helps me build credibility, helps refine my presentation skills, and builds relationships in the community so I can be more effective at what I do.

Sales experts will tell you that the details and process of selling a service or product is the least important and effective part of sales. Developing a strong network, helping others, providing solutions, and delivering value, building credibility and consumer confidence, are much more important to overall business growth and success (see Figure 3.5).

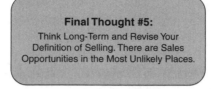

Final Thought #5:
Think Long-Term and Revise Your Definition of Selling. There are Sales Opportunities in the Most Unlikely Places.

Figure 3.5   Revise Your Definition of Selling

Be Visible and Accessible

A great measure of success in business is becoming a part of the collective consciousness of the community and/or market you serve. One way to accomplish this is by ensuring you are in front of your target audience as much as possible.

Developing effective communication vehicles to reach clients and offering services and products that are of value to the community are powerful tools for building credibility and making an impression.

Top performing sales professionals use this concept and method often and with much success. I recall a time when a colleague e-mailed me a free article on a topic that was directly related to the work we were both doing as sales professionals. I read the article and was very impressed with the content and amazed that it was being offered free of charge. So I looked on the person's web site and read about his service offerings, which included workshops, books, and additional products. I wasn't willing to buy anything at that time but I liked the fact he offered free products that benefited me, and there was an invitation to join his mailing list to receive his free newsletter and updates about other free products. So I joined and thought nothing more of it or him for weeks. Three weeks later I received an e-mail from him offering two free audio clips on topics that I found very interesting. I listened to both audio clips, took notes, and was grateful for the new information. But once again, I thought nothing more of him. Three weeks later I was knee-deep in work on a project when I received an e-mail promoting this person's new book. I previewed the content and loved the topic because it spoke directly to what I was working on at the time. I thought it would help me immensely and decided to purchase the book. I enjoyed it tremendously, so much so that I purchased a more extensive workshop series that was much more expensive.

Can You See What I Am Getting At Here?

There is tremendous power in putting yourself in front of potential clients. One of the best ways to do this is to offer people things that will help them. This goes back to the principle of value as I define it: *Offering a service or product with no expectation of something in return.* This keeps you present in people's minds and builds a certain level of credibility so that people will seek you out when they need help.

Do You See the Power of Using Systems?
This person used today's technology to be available to me so I would buy when the time was right. He built credibility through the quality of his free offerings and then remained visible. His approach was highly effective. He generated word-of-mouth marketing whereby other people were promoting his services and products by sharing it with work colleagues and friends. And he created a buying environment simply by making himself a resource and being easily accessible in a way that was non-threatening and non-intrusive.

This concept is incredibly relevant within the mental health industry. We need to be ready and available when people are in crisis and need help. Who do they turn to when they are having problems? Who do they seek out when they have a question or concern that they believe might require clinical services? Hopefully, the answer is you.

Summary

- Move away from the selling process and become part of the buying process. Create a shift where people seek you out to buy what you are selling. A customer-focused sales model will help you make this all-important shift.
- Focus on your customers' needs and learn to sell the way people want to buy. Offer solutions and not simply features.
- Solution-oriented selling shifts the spotlight from you, the seller, to the potential customer/client.
- A distinguishing skill of top performing sales professionals is their ability to ask thoughtful questions of prospects. Use your mental health skills to listen to customer needs and ask questions that get at the core of their wants.
- Position yourself as a trusted resource in the community by finding unique ways to offer value to customers. Reread this chapter to review techniques and exercises that will help you build value.
- Learn and adopt these five principles that will help build your reputation and build visibility.
  1. Give to others as often as possible.
  2. Give others credit and make others look good.
  3. Be better prepared than your competitors.
  4. Over-deliver and always follow through.
  5. Think long-term and treat everyone as a customer because they are!

PART TWO

The Psychology of Success

CHAPTER FOUR

Finding Your Power

The Social Dynamics of Power, Influence, and Persuasion

"I'm gonna make him an offer he can't refuse."

—*Don Corleone*, The Godfather

Most mental health practitioners rarely, if ever, examine the role of social dynamics as a psychological force within their own work environment. It is such a new concept in the field that I would venture a guess that the mere mention of social dynamics would be interpreted solely to mean the role practitioners play in the clinical process. Clinicians study phenomena such as the importance of nonverbal communication and the role of power/perception within the confines of a therapeutic relationship, but they rarely turn an eye toward the impact of these phenomena on their own business successes and failures. In the world of business, social dynamics involving power, control, and influence play a significant role and often determine positive or negative outcomes. Buying decisions, strategic alliances, and other business activities are influenced greatly by how people judge a situation and how they view you as a business professional. Right or wrong, we all make these judgments, and they, in turn, greatly influence our behavior and future decisions.

In the real world, hierarchical power structures permeate all social systems in an attempt to provide structure and order. People existing within these systems inevitably bring their own unique positions, biases, personalities, and strengths to the table. Your unique attributes, in turn, contribute to your influential power and the impact you may have within an existing environment and social structure. Make no mistake about it, we all practice some form of persuasion and influence every single day of our lives. Sometimes it is intentional, and at other times it is an entirely unconscious phenomenon.

Now let me propose a hypothetical situation. What if you became more aware of these dynamics within your place of employment? What if you were able to use this newfound awareness to create an environment where you were in a position of strength and credibility in the eyes of a potential client? Few people realize that sales success in any industry involves understanding that selling is a game of psychological positioning and persuasion. Those who position themselves most effectively are the ones who earn the power and ability to manage the decision making process for the consumer. Use these principles in a smart and efficient manner, and you have the competitive advantage.

This chapter takes a closer look at the influential psychodynamics of power and control in business settings, and the role it plays in determining success and failure. It is intended to teach you how to gain power and influence in your marketing and sales efforts so you may prosper in whatever mental health career path you choose to follow.

This topic may make you feel a bit uncomfortable. It may even make you question whether you are being manipulative and/or functioning in a manner that is counter to your mission as a helping professional. But I assure you that there are jewels of wisdom and knowledge within these concepts. We cannot simply ignore the power systems and structures operating in our lives, as they are an essential component of every social system. And when you take a closer look, you will find that adopting these principles simply means utilizing influential behavior and power to give people the psychological freedom to benefit from something they may really want or need.

So before moving forward, I ask once again that you set aside your beliefs and/or notions about power, perception, and control in order to look closely at the conscious and unconscious phenomena impacting business practice on a daily basis.

What Does "Power" Mean and Why Does it Matter for Your Practice?

There is some dispute among researchers as to the relationship between power, influence, and persuasion. **Power** at its most basic level can be defined as the potential to make and enforce decisions. **Influence** differs from power in that it is the vehicle people use to exert power. **Persuasion** is closely linked to influence. However, it has differences in that it does not involve use of coercion, which is the case with some influential behavior. Persuasion is a process whereby someone attempts to change a belief or attitude of an individual or group. In many cases, persuasion is a mutually beneficial process, and it is used effectively by most top performing business executives.

In 1959, researchers John R.P. French Jr. and Bertram Raven examined and studied the concept of power in various social settings. Their efforts led to a theory that identifies five bases of social and organizational power (a sixth base was added later). Within these bases is the belief that the processes involved in power are complex and often disguised in our society. Consequently, those who are better able to understand and become aware of power bases and dynamics are in a better position to manage and prosper within specific hierarchical social structures.

The six bases are as follows:

1. **Reward power:**
   This form of power exists when a person believes, correctly or incorrectly, that you control a reward system that they have the ability to earn.

2. **Coercive power:**
   Coercive power is related to how much a person can be punished by you and the extent to which that person believes this punishment can be avoided by complying with your directives.

3. **Expert power:**
   Within this power base, your power is the direct result of people's perception that you possess special knowledge and expertise.

4. **Legitimate power:**
   The impact of legitimate power comes from people's belief that you have the legal authority to influence them in some way.

5. **Referent power:**
   This power is based on how much someone likes you as an individual. This person may be drawn to your communication style, your personality, charisma, or confidence. The transference phenomenon may also play a significant role as your power over another may be a function of how much you are able to influence another person's feelings of personal acceptance, approval, and self-esteem.

6. **Information Power:**
   This power base is the result of one's ability to control information needed by others in order to reach an important goal.

These forms of power are used or experienced by all of us at some point in time, and they often lead to different outcomes. In business, there are times when coercive power is essential to bringing about movement and resolving issues. C-Level executives use their positions of power and authority to bring about order and to ensure that effective and timely decisions are made for the good of the organization. Private practitioners use their power as experts in specific fields to win business, to make clinical decisions, and to drive the treatment process.

The initial goal regarding this discussion is to become more aware of power dynamics within your social networks and to begin to recognize the different bases of power that are being adopted by those you come into contact with as you go about your day. This awareness step will begin to give you insight into how power dynamics impact you and how you use your own power in specific settings.

Now that we have identified and defined these concepts, a logical question for many of you might be, *"How can I use these forms of power to position myself effectively in the marketplace?"* It starts with making an effort to level the playing field, which I describe here.

Personal Power

Every business interaction involves the use of the principles of power, influence, and persuasion. They are critical components to help achieve goals and objectives at all levels. In addition, virtually every social interaction involves some form of negotiation that is in essence a sales opportunity.

We can identify numerous examples in all areas of life, but for our purposes, here are a few that directly relate to the mental health profession.

- When new clients come to your private practice, they receive and process information and immediately form impressions about your credibility and whether or not they will benefit from your services. They analyze everything from the first hello to the look and feel of your office.
- You may work for a large organization and you are designated to be the leader of an important internal project. Part of that assignment involves gaining buy-in from others in order to overcome obstacles, accomplish tasks, and achieve success. In addition, you will need to possess a degree of power and utilize your influence to make decisions that will move the project forward. Your colleagues' perception of you as a competent project leader will strongly determine the level of support and assistance you receive.
- If you are looking for a new job opportunity, one of your primary tasks will be to identify an approach that will convince others of your value. If they perceive you as being someone who can fulfill a need within their business, then the power shifts from the organization to you, the candidate. They begin pursuing you and make an effort to give you an offer you will accept.

What is notable within these examples is the importance of perception and the role of power and influence in determining success. Research in the area of power, influence, and social dynamics shows that within any interaction there is one party who holds the majority of power. The person who possesses that power is the one who ultimately controls the process, flow, and outcome of that interaction.

People's Perceptions are Your Reality

When I talk about the role of perception in human interactions, along with the idea of harnessing power and control in the work environment, I'm referring specifically to the importance of being aware that social positioning, social value, power, and control are present at varying degrees in all interactions, and they often exist at an unconscious level. If you become aware of these phenomena in your daily interactions, you will be able to work more effectively within the hierarchical system that is present at that time. You will see the dynamics at play and will begin to recognize those moments when you have inadvertently given up your power. Recognize these patterns, and you will begin to take back your personal power. The idea here is not to achieve power through manipulative tactics but to recognize the role of effective positioning and the impact sub-communication has within the workplace. Your recognition of these concepts gives you the ability to change specific behaviors within yourself and to use client-focused sales concepts to earn a positive position of power and influence.

Who Holds the Power and How to Level the Playing Field in Our Profession

As you strive to grow your practice and career, you may notice that there are occasions when you're in a weaker position than that of the customer/prospect who you are trying to convince to use your services. This is especially true if you are relatively new to the field. Why is this the case? There are many factors and perhaps the most important of these is the concept of **greatest need**.

Essentially, the person with the greatest need is the one who relinquishes his or her power to another. As a result, if you have not demonstrated your value to the customer, then you have unknowingly placed that person in the ultimate position of power. Whether you have done this consciously makes no difference. What matters is that the customer has perceived you as being the one in need. When this happens, your chances of earning his or her business greatly diminish.

How do you change this? *The key in the beginning is positioning!* You must take steps to position yourself in the community where you offer tremendous value and are highly visible within your target market. You do this by adopting the client-focused sales principles and new marketing concepts discussed throughout this book so that people begin to seek you out for services and assistance.

The world of professional sales offers us an important lesson with regard to the relationship between customer need and power. The biggest differentiating factor between top performing sales professionals and those who struggle has to do with the awareness of power dynamics and the ability to create need through value-based services or products. Top performers recognize the relationship between need and power in business situations, and they have the ability to obtain and use this power throughout the negotiation process. The same holds true for the mental health industry. Those who create the greatest need and keep a certain level of authority and credibility are the ones who will be most successful.

Exploring Power Dynamics: A Mental Health Example

Let's use an example from the world of mental health to explore this process further. Suppose you are an experienced clinician looking to grow your business by choosing to offer additional workshops for the community. You develop a variety of workshops on troubled adolescents and parenting skills. You contact various organizations asking to advertise your service offerings, and as a result, you are given an opportunity to speak at a PTA meeting of 40 to 50 families in the community. On the day of the meeting you arrive and are given 15 minutes at the beginning of the meeting to talk about who you are and what services you offer. You develop some nice brochures and leave them for people who might be interested. Who has the power in this scenario? What are some of the power dynamics? Hold that thought for a moment.

Contrast this with a slightly different scenario in which the local PTA identifies an increasing problem concerning adolescent violence and other risky behaviors that are having a negative impact in the community. A PTA attendee mentions that there is a clinician in the area who has done research on the topic of risky behaviors for adolescents. That clinician is you. They contact you and ask you to speak on the subject matter. You are positioned as the featured event on the agenda for the evening. You give a brief training on the topic and open the floor for questions, which leads to a lengthy question and answer period. Following this discussion you inform the audience of your intent to start a new educational group for parents on how to address problematic behaviors in adolescents.

These two scenarios are vastly different when we look at the dynamics of power, persuasion, and need. In the initial scenario you are clearly in a weaker position than the audience. The simple fact that you approached them about attending one of their meetings immediately placed you in a more subservient and weaker position. In addition, you had no differentiating factors, meaning there was no credibility or awareness building generated about your services and expertise. You were simply viewed as one of many clinicians in the community coming to them to ask for their business. You were just another face in the crowd. As a result, you had very little influence and no control over the process. The audience would hold the power throughout the interaction, and they would be the ones to determine the outcome of the meeting.

In the latter example you were immediately put into a position of strength and credibility because the group contacted you about a specific need and believed you had the ability to meet that need. As a result, the relational dynamics were vastly different. You would step to the podium in front of an audience that did not need to be convinced or sold. You would be seen as someone with answers, someone who could solve their problems. They were, in essence, willing buyers in this scenario, and therefore, you would have much more control over the situation and would be able to manage the meeting in order to achieve a particular outcome. Research shows that this position inevitably leads to higher sales success rates.

There are numerous examples that can demonstrate the presence and importance of power and control in determining business success. The goal for all of you in the profession is to identify ways to *level the playing field* or, better yet, to *transcend* it so you operate from a position of strength. Watch and see the results when you begin making this effort.

TRANSLATING POWER INTO INFLUENCE AND SUCCESS

Power is often exhibited and revealed through a person's ability to use influential tactics and techniques. An important next step in the discussion of power is to identify ways in which you can translate this power into highly effective forms of influential behavior.

What follows is a discussion of cutting edge principles and techniques based on time-tested psychological principles of human behavior. These are incredibly powerful principles of influence that will bring about dramatic results for you.

Using the Power of Groups

There are numerous historical examples, both good and bad, of the power and influence of the majority. Groups can be highly influential to the point where others will put aside their initial impressions based on the overarching opinions of the group. Can you recall a time when you were highly influenced by the opinion, position, or actions of the majority? Was it difficult to hold onto your initial impressions? Did you question your own viewpoint in light of what the group believed?

So what in the world does a discussion about the power of the majority have to do with your role as a mental health professional? Well, let's begin to put what we have learned thus far about power and influence to good use within our profession. If we know and understand that people tend to gravitate toward groups and are highly influenced by the power of the majority, it would stand to reason that a highly effective selling strategy for you would be to identify and foster a group of your own.

A great first step would involve making an effort to define your group, meaning identifying and reaching out to those people who have used your services and benefited from them. This group will serve as your "promotional group." If used correctly, this group of people can be very powerful and will possess a high level of influence over others in the marketplace. Keep them connected with you in some way, whether it be through free service offerings, mailer updates, or volunteer services in the community. This concept is very much in line with the new marketing models discussed earlier in the book. The key is to identify and nurture your own group so that you can call on them when the time comes. When you begin to market your services out in the community, I recommend that you aggressively gather information about your promotional group and display this information through testimonials and success stories so that everyone can see. If you are able to define, build, and grow your own group, a group that believes in you and supports you, then future clients will follow their lead.

Let's look at this concept another way. Suppose you are a clinician offering what you believe to be outstanding mental health services. Over the years, numerous people and their families have used and benefited from your help. If this is the case for you, find ways to show potential clients that others have gained tremendous satisfaction and healing from your services. If you do this effectively, the potential clients will tend to follow the lead of the group, and the chances of someone choosing to use your services will increase dramatically. Always remember, it is human nature to make decisions based on the opinion and input from a group rather than taking the risk of going it alone.

Forming and defining your own promotional group will not only increase the likelihood of potential clients choosing to do business with you, but it will also positively influence their satisfaction after they use your service! That's right, people will be influenced by the majority before, during, and after they have utilized your services.

Have you ever dined at a restaurant known for having the best food in your local area or attended a concert given by a musician whom the world recognized as historically significant? I would bet the group who identified them as being the best influenced your impressions of the food or the performance at the concert. Sure, the concert may have been excellent but hearing from others that the musician was the best in decades made it that much better! The reason for this has to do with the fact that when you use a service or purchase a product, your expectations are molded somewhat by the group, which serves to enhance your overall experience.

The take-away for you with regard to the power of the majority is to begin to use this power to your advantage by defining your own promotional group and utilizing their incredible influence to improve on your success.

Opening the Door to Bigger Opportunities

I learned early on in my career about the power and relevance of achieving something small as a stepping-stone to much grander opportunities. Top-level sales professionals understand and use this concept brilliantly, and we can all benefit from their knowledge and skill in this area.

I recall one such sales expert whom I first heard about through a colleague. My friend suggested I look at this person's web site, as he was offering a free book I could download. I could not believe it! What a steal, I thought. Here was one of the best-recognized people in his industry offering me an 80-page book on a topic I found extremely interesting. What I did not realize at the time was the fact that he was guiding me through a sales process focused on long-term growth and results. I certainly knew there was some promotional intent behind his offering, but I found his material to be well done so I signed up to be on his mailing list just in case he offered some other excellent free stuff! What occurred was something entirely different. This small step of getting me to visit his site led to my downloading and reading his book, registering to be on his mailing list, and eventually purchasing many of his product offerings. To this day I continue to purchase his products, as they continue to give me great value and benefit.

This experience encapsulates another key psychological principle of influence: The most important step toward getting someone to choose to use your service or buy your product is to get people to agree to small things first. The bigger opportunities will come later.

This influential technique is based on the sales progression model discussed in Chapter 2. The idea here is to engage people first and gain their interest by offering quality resources and valuable information free of charge. You build influence by earning trust. And how is trust earned? In many cases, people want to experience what you offer. Offering people a low risk, no cost opportunity gives them a chance to learn more about you. And if they have a positive first impression they will be much more likely to take the next step.

Once again, let's put this into terms that speak directly to those in the mental health profession. Suppose a psychotherapist in private practice decides to offer free one-page fact and resource sheets for families around the issue of Pervasive Developmental Disorders (PDD). This therapist gives the information to a friend who works in the school system, thereby opening the door just a little bit. A family gets hold of this reference sheet and finds it extremely helpful and useful for relating to their child. They make a point of thanking the school principal for offering this information, which leads to a discussion about who offered the information in the first place. Before long, the entire County learns of the PDD resource sheet, and the psychotherapist receives high praise for his or her expertise and support of the community. Eventually, the therapist is asked to give several speeches to families across the county about social skill development with adolescent age children. He or she becomes recognized within the school system as someone teachers and guidance counselors should refer families to when there are mental health problems or concerns. The end result is a consistent referral resource that helps to grow his or her practice by leaps and bounds!

Hopefully, you can see the sales progression in these examples. It is also important to note that the idea of offering something for free is an effective sales technique *only* if you have a good plan for going from opening the door to uncovering wealth building opportunities. You must define a step-by-step plan for guiding a potential client to the next step of the buying process, and you must have the ability to deliver at each step. The sales expert who earned my business had a process where I went from visiting his site to taking a deeper level of action by downloading his book so that I eventually began purchasing his products.

As you work toward building your practice and growing your career, look for small windows of opportunity and small commitments first. Once the door is unlocked it is much easier to get inside.

The Intrigue of the Unfinished: Using Teaser Campaigns to Build Business

People have a difficult time when something is left undone. For most of us, there is a desire to bring closure to an unfinished thought or idea. We become more engaged in the idea presented and begin searching for ways to fully understand and complete the idea, thought, or concept.

Now stay with me here because the information I am about to tell you next is the most important of all for determining success in the profession. It is the crown jewel of all the principles presented in this book for one major reason. . . . .

Okay, could you begin to feel a change from within as you were reading the last two sentences? Were you anxiously or excitedly moving forward to find out how the last sentence would be completed?

Essentially, I created an engaging moment that was enhanced further by the fact that I left something unfinished. Just when you were about to get to an important point I ended the thought, which in turn increased your desire to take action in order to complete the thought and reveal the answer. In this case the action was turning to the next page. It would have been very difficult to choose to close this book right after the unfinished sentence. This phenomenon is extremely valuable in the world of marketing. When used properly it provides you with a psychological edge that will engage people and get them to move closer to making a decision to use your services.

Teaser Campaigns in Mental Health

Let's look at a mental health example to further clarify the power of this influential technique. Suppose I choose to advertise a new workshop that is designed to empower people to create richer and more meaningful lives for themselves. I might post a statement on my web site or as a printed advertisement. It might look something like this:

> "Do you find yourself stuck in a rut where life seems to lack meaning and fulfillment? There are seven key steps to enriching your life in ways you may not have imagined. Are you utilizing all of these principles?"

Or you might try this:

> "Are you finding yourself feeling down on a daily basis? Do you wake up in the morning dreading the day to come? There are powerful solutions, and they can be employed now to produce immediate results. To find out more about these solutions contact Joe Smith at 777–7777."

Take a look at your marketing efforts, and begin to think of ways in which you can employ this principle of influence in order to compel people to see who you are and to explore what you do. This technique is a powerful way to engage people and to move them through your sales process.

The Use of Framing in the Mental Health Profession

One Saturday afternoon while driving with my family, my wife began talking about an advertisement in a free local quarterly guide she picked up earlier in the day that piqued her interest. "Listen to this," she said to me as she began reading statements asking the female reader if she had ever uttered these words:

"I feel like I'm going crazy"

"Who is this person in my body?"

"If he says that to me one more time, I'm going to rip his head off."

She chuckled as she read the ad and then went on about what the family says in response to a woman's behavior and/or attitude…

"Mommy, you are so mean."

"You need to chill out."

"You need to get some help."

This time she laughed and then told me to keep listening as the advertisement ended with an explanation of what the reader typically does…

"You run yourself ragged taking care of everyone else."

"You scream at your kids, then you feel guilty."

"You take antidepressants, but you are still depressed."

The ad then went on to ensure readers that they were not alone and that they were *not crazy*. Following this was a brief discussion about the relationship between hormones and the specific feelings and behaviors identified in the advertisement. The ad concluded with a statement about the kinds of programs and services available that went beyond psychotropic medications and psychotherapy.

This was an extremely effective and powerful advertisement created by a woman who worked to alleviate these symptoms through hormone therapy. She was able to talk about life situations and circumstances in a manner that spoke to my wife and in a way that made sense in terms of how her services could help with some of the problem areas identified. What she used effectively was an influential tactic known as **framing**.

A frame is a mental window through which we view reality or a particular problem. In most instances, we frame reality in terms of our own unique issues, interests, and beliefs. So, as an example, a woman dealing with the many demands of being a mother, wife, and professional might see her increasing frustration as a problem she needs to simply deal with silently. She may think to herself, working mothers have been juggling these demands successfully for years. Or perhaps a woman reading this advertisement views these problems on a psychological level and believes they require some form of counseling or behavioral intervention. What the woman who posted the ad was able to do so effectively for the reader was *reframe* the problem or problems in a manner that compelled the person to see that perhaps there were other factors involved and other solutions.

This is a good example of framing an issue to influence the outcome. It involves recognizing and speaking to the emotional triggers, wants, and needs of others in order to change people's perceptions and to influence the decision making process. In this case, hormone therapy or consultation might be a more effective intervention than other competing services such as psychotherapy and psychiatric intervention.

I have seen many examples of people who have effectively used framing to gain power and influence. I recall one therapist in my community who was excellent at the technique of framing. His skill in this regard gave him access to markets that other therapists could not penetrate — simply because he was so effective at using this approach. He would often speak with certain groups and communities who had a significant level of resistance and prejudice toward psychotherapy. They viewed therapy as a weakness or as something that offered them little to no value. However, once they heard from this thera-pist, their viewpoint typically shifted. He was able to do this in much the same manner as the woman who posted the advertisement promoting hormone ther-apy. He used examples common to many people that elicited strong emotional responses and that helped to capture the audience's attention. He was then able to bring about a shift in their frame of reference by explaining how his approach to counseling would positively affect these problems in highly practi-cal and life changing ways.

In summary, improving on your ability to frame a situation so people are able to see your reality or your point of view can go a long way to uncovering opportunities. Therefore, take time to understand "hot issues" that will engage others and lead to a shift in awareness on the part of the consumer.

Understanding How People Make Purchasing Decisions

Many years ago a well-known retailer introduced a new high-end product. It was the best the company had to offer and naturally, the most expensive. When they introduced this item, they were expecting to reach a small niche customer base. However, what occurred, and what the retailer witnessed, was an entirely different phenomenon altogether. Sales for the old item that was replaced in both price and prestige more than doubled immediately upon introduction of the newer higher-end item. In less than a few months the retailer sold more of the older item than they had the entire year prior. What happened? The answer can be found when one has a better understanding of the psychology of customer choice, and it offers some interesting insights into how to go to market with the services you provide.

Behavioral scientists of all persuasions find that when customers consider a particular set of choices *(services or products)*, they tend to favor alternatives that are so-called compromise choices. These are choices that fall between what a person needs at a minimum, and what they could possibly spend and fully desire at a maximum.

Therefore, when people must make a decision between only two products or two services, they often compromise by opting for a service that seems more doable in their minds. And if there is only one option offered, then the customer's decision may be to simply look elsewhere for help.

What is even more interesting to note is what happens when a third service option is introduced. When presented with a third option that is even more expensive than the other two, the previous high-end choice shifts to become the moderately priced service.

"Boy, I would love to have that product with all the bells and whistles, but it is just too expensive. I can always opt for the lower-end model, but what about this middle option here? It offers more than the lower-end option, and I can still get a lot of the great features I want without breaking the bank. I think this middle option would be the best choice."

This restructured set of options that puts the former high-end choice in the middle inevitably draws people to this option. And why not? It offers more than the lower-end service with the added benefit of being more cost-effective than the high-end choice.

In this way, high-end products provide some very important benefits for your mental health business:

- They offer top-of-line and all-encompassing services that meet the high-end needs of a small group of current and future customers.
- They change the customer choice model by offering an additional option. This serves to not only expand your services but to make them more attractive to customers based on the psychology of customer choice.

Researchers also note that the elimination of a high-end or expensive service offering may actually have a negative domino effect on other areas of your business. You may have very good reasons for getting rid of a service (e.g., limited use due to cost). But remember, removing it as an option will reposition another of your services to the high-end role, and this may actually lead to a reduction in usage of that service as well.

If you offer workshops, individual psychotherapy, coaching, or group therapy services, you may want to examine whether you have a good balance of service offerings. You don't want to offer too many options as this may confuse and deter people. However, too few options also prove limiting and restrictive. Your best strategy is to offer three to four good choices for a specific service or product. This helps to frame your services and gives people an opportunity to make a more informed choice.

As an example, if you're delivering a two-day workshop you might want to consider giving people a few additional choices. Studies show that this increases attendance significantly. Offer a full two-day program at $150 per person on one end of the spectrum (complete with a workbook and all the bells and whistles) and an $80 first day only program on the other end. And in between, consider offering a mid-level service in both price and substance so that more people are given an opportunity to benefit from what you have to offer.

You can use this approach to lay out a variety of service and product offerings regardless of what you do in the field.

PRACTICAL TECHNIQUES FOR USING PERSONAL POWER EFFECTIVELY

One of the best ways to maintain a high level of influence is to avoid behavior that puts you in subservient and supplicating roles. What most do not realize is just how relevant the role of perception is within our social and professional interactions. How we behave and interact with others can convey many things to a potential client. If you portray a sense of confidence through your behaviors, many people will be comforted by their belief that you will be able to care for them and address their needs. Now think of a time in your life when you met with someone about a need and that person did not exude confidence. There was just something about that person that made you uncomfortable and made you wonder how you could remove yourself from the situation. Can you remember times when this happened to you? Chances are, in those instances, you did not want to buy whatever that person was selling!

In this section I briefly discuss and review some practical nonverbal and verbal communication tips and techniques that will help you hold onto personal power.

Nonverbal Cues

For many years now researchers have studied and stressed the power of nonverbal communication. Research in this area finds that over 90% of our communication is based on our nonverbal cues. Yes, as mental health professionals we all know this to be the case, but do we practice this in our daily lives? Here are some good examples of nonverbal cues that negatively affect personal power.

- *Lack of eye contact.* In most cases, those in positions of authority tend to do a better job of using eye contact effectively. Studies in the area of professional sales communicate the importance of holding appropriate eye contact to instill a sense of confidence and control during negotiations. Other studies show that those in weaker positions of authority use less eye contact with a superior than with someone who is deemed their equal by virtue of their social status. They are also the first ones to look away from the person they are talking with, and this also serves to establish a social hierarchy.

In the mental health field clinicians conducting an initial assessment will note level and use of eye contact as an important clue in terms of sense of self-worth and feelings of discomfort and anxiety. It is important to use eye contact effectively so that you can gain and hold onto a certain level of power and influence.

- *Closing yourself off.*

When you take up too little space or you sit in a closed position you create the appearance of someone who is worried about infringing on the space of another. It communicates on a deeper level that you feel inferior to another and when you do this, naturally you set up a social dynamic where the other person or persons are in a stronger position precisely because you have given them this power. The reality is that people with power take up space and stake their claim to wherever they are at that moment. Try it sometime! The next time you go to a business meeting avoid the temptation to take as little space as possible. Find yourself a prime spot at the table and give yourself room to be. Then observe the group dynamics and see how this new position affects the hierarchical structure of the group.

- *Leaning in.*

I realize that in some clinical settings leaning in is a technique used to show interest in the patient, however, in many other situations it can be viewed as a supplicating behavior where you are deferring to the power of another. Remember that the purpose here is to discuss the impact nonverbal behaviors have on your personal power and ultimately your ability to sell yourself and your services. Therefore, always remember that leaning in to the speaker automatically creates a power differential that does not stand in your favor.

Verbal Cues

Not too long ago my colleagues and I were speaking over the phone with a potential out-of-state vendor about the possibility of developing a web site for our organization. We were looking at a handful of candidates, most of whom we met face-to-face since they were from our local area. As a result, it seemed that this vendor would be at a significant disadvantage trying to sell his services. Turns out he won our business without ever meeting us in person, and this was due in large part to how he presented himself during the conference call. He had a calming influence; he did a great job of listening to our needs; and he was able to provide honest and succinct answers that exuded a sense of confidence in his abilities. He did not seem overeager like many of the other candidates. In fact, it was very clear that while he would love to work with us, he did not need our business; and it was this position that gave him a level of credibility and influence.

A few days later we met with another web developer and the dynamics were significantly different. This group appeared overeager and needy. As a result, our team felt somewhat uncomfortable during the meeting. As the meeting progressed, it became apparent that they had their own agenda; and this got in the way of their ability to hear our concerns and understand our needs. At one point I recall that they shifted focus and told us that, in their professional opinion, we needed a suite of marketing services and, not surprisingly, they had the ability to meet all those needs!

We interviewed a third organization; and before we could even begin the meeting, they spent 30 minutes telling us about all their accomplishments without any concern for our needs and how they proposed to meet those needs. This organization lost all power and influence before they ever began discussing how their services would help solve our problems.

The developer who won our business presented much differently than his two main competitors. He was thoughtful in his responses; he asked great follow-up questions that showed he was listening; and he was completely honest about what he was and was not able to do. He was able to accomplish all of this over the phone using excellent verbal skills that were incredibly powerful and convincing.

Here are just a few of these verbal skills worth noting:

- *Control the meeting by setting clear boundaries and staying focused.*

When you are selling a service, facilitating a meeting, or giving a presentation, be sure to stick to your agenda. If others ask questions, politely tell them you will get to their question once you finish your current presentation or discussion. The most common thing to do in these situations is to attempt to immediately respond to the prompts of others, thereby veering off course and losing your focus. Shifting your focus quickly and often comes across as being overeager and needy. In addition, many people in attendance will become frustrated by your inability to manage the meeting. A more powerful position to take is one in which you set clear boundaries and remain focused.

The web developer we spoke with over the phone was very sophisticated in this regard. He was presented with an initial request about our need for a new web site, so when he was interrupted with a question, he politely thanked the person for asking the question and then said he wanted to be sure he addressed our initial overarching needs first and he would be happy to discuss other issues later. His responses were commanding but not arrogant, powerful but not pushy or abrupt. One thing was very clear — he was in charge of the meeting, and this reality was a relief for our team, as we did not have to work to get what we wanted. He was going to do the work for us so we could make the best choice possible.

- *Slow down and use more deliberate speech.*

One of the biggest mistakes people make when they first start selling something is to talk fast and furiously. This is another way in which you can lose power and credibility quickly. In the world of professional sales, people who are worried that they will be rejected or cut off by a potential client tend to talk too quickly in an effort to get as much information communicated as possible before this occurs.

The person we chose to develop our web site spoke in a calm, relaxed, and confident manner. When questions were asked he often paused for a moment and then began to address the question in a deliberate manner. The message it conveyed to our team was that this person was thoughtful, patient, and competent. As a result, we felt very confident he would do an excellent job for our organization.

I suggest taking some time to notice when you are rushing your speech and begin making an effort to slow down, relax, and confidently present your point. This is an excellent way to maintain power and influence.

- *Avoid losing your voice.*

What I am referring to here is not the literal concept of "losing your voice," but rather when a person's voice loses its power at the end of a sentence or statement. Let me explain further.

Think of a time when you were speaking with a person or group of people, and you were not feeling very confident or secure. During those moments, did you notice that your voice lost its strength near the end of a sentence as if your words began to disappear into thin air? Many people fall victim to this, but are unaware of its occurrence or relevance. In these instances your voice begins clearly. However, as you continue it softens, and the words near the end trail off and are unintelligible to the listener. Pay attention to your speech patterns, and see if you fall victim to this under certain conditions. Chances are that this occurs during those times when you are feeling uncomfortable.

Professional speakers pay particular attention to this concept because they know it communicates weakness to the listener and a general lack of confidence in oneself. Remember this during job interviews, when you are selling a service, or when you are giving a presentation to your leadership team, and make an effort to end your statements with impact and power!

THOUGHTS TO KEEP IN MIND

Remember that a healthy awareness of the reality and presence of power and influence can have a dramatic impact on the overall success of your business. Understand the role power plays in your profession, and use some of the practical techniques we have discussed to improve your own power, influence, and persuasion.

SUMMARY

- Sales success in any industry involves understanding the role of psychological positioning and persuasion in everyday interactions. People's perception and interpretation of your position of power will have a significant impact on your ability to sell yourself and your services.
- Every social interaction involves some form of negotiation that is, in essence, a sales opportunity.
- Social positioning, social value, power, and control are present at varying degrees in all interactions. The person with the greatest need is the one who relinquishes his or her power to another. Use various tools and techniques presented in this chapter to be in a position of strength during business interactions.
- Some important marketing concepts worth noting are: leveraging the power of groups; learning to open small doors that lead to greater opportunity; using the intrigue of the incomplete; and the art of framing. Review this chapter for details about these principles.

- Understand the psychology of customer choice and use this approach whenever you go to market with a new service offering. It will dramatically increase your response rates and usage.
- Nonverbal and verbal messages you use every day play a significant role in determining your position of power in personal interactions. Use those that are beneficial, and work to get rid of common ways of interacting that will place you in a lesser role.

CHAPTER FIVE

Finding Your Place in the Field

Effective Strategies for Building Credibility and Earning Authority

From 1961through 1963 a Yale University psychologist named Stanley Milgram conducted a series of sociological studies focusing on the conflict between obedience to authority and personal conscience. The outcomes of these studies led to some surprising and important findings pertaining to influential power and the importance of authority.

In brief, college students volunteered to participate in a research study about the effect of punishment on learning and memory. Or so they thought! Students were met by a man wearing a lab coat and carrying a clipboard; in plain view another man was sitting in a glass room with electrodes attached to his head and body. The students were unaware that the man in the glass room was a paid actor. As the experiment began, the lab technician informed the students he would be asking the man in the glass room a series of questions, and if the man answered a question incorrectly, he would instruct the student to administer a shock as a form of aversive stimuli. The shock, of course, would never actually occur, but it would certainly appear to the students that it was administered, as evidenced by the painful reaction of the paid actor in the glass room. With each wrong answer the intensity of the shock would increase. As the experiment progressed, students would supply the shock, and the actor's painful reaction would intensify significantly. The experiment continued to move forward, and it became more and more apparent that the shocks were now seriously harming the man in the glass room. In spite of this knowledge, students continued to follow the directives of the lab technician.

The results of the experiment surprised everyone. Not until the volunteer was in extreme pain and stated he could no longer provide answers did anyone participating in the experiment choose to stop, and even then only a few actually did so. Amazingly, 65% of the students participating in the experiment were willing to go even farther and administer shock voltages that would have been fatal to the volunteer had they been real.

The study was replicated using several different populations and has been repeated over the years by other psychologists around the world with similar results. Milgram concluded that the overall results of the study had to do with the incredible power that perceived authority had over each participant (Milgram, 1963). Participants in the study were significantly influenced by the identified authority figure in the study and were willing to obey his directives in spite of the physical harm inflicted on another.

This study not only provides evidence about the power and influence of authority, it also reveals just how important it is to build credibility and earn a certain level of authority within your profession. There are few things in the world of business that will get you more clients and beat out your competition better than being recognized as an expert in your field.

As the Milgram study suggests, being viewed as an authority figure in some way, shape, or form creates a vastly different perception and image of you in the eyes of the community, and this perception can either help or hinder your success, depending on which side of the credibility continuum you fall on.

How do you leverage your expertise? There are numerous ways and in this chapter, you will be presented with specific strategies and techniques that will help you to build credibility, earn authority, and position yourself as an expert in your field.

BUILDING A FOUNDATION FOR PROFESSIONAL SUCCESS

After graduate school I took an entry-level clinical position and entered the profession full of excitement and optimism. Unfortunately, years passed and I never found the spark or passion that would propel me to bigger and better things in the field. Oh, I could create some sort of excuse and say I was new to the field and still finding my way, but the fact of the matter was that I had been presented with numerous opportunities to learn, study, and grow as a clinician and simply chose not to take the challenge. As a result, I would come to work, do what I was asked, and then leave as quickly as possible to pursue other interests. The impact of this approach was profound. I became competent in several clinical areas but never excelled in any particular discipline. A person who had a mental health problem certainly would not have sought me out for clinical advice, because my skill level and range was no different than that of the majority. I simply did not have the depth or breadth of knowledge that would launch me into greater opportunity and career growth.

This dilemma was much more significant than I realized at the time. For instance, I had some experience with substance abuse treatment and I could facilitate recovery groups, but if you wanted a presentation on a specific area of substance abuse treatment or an expert in the field to provide consultation services, I was not your man. I could also provide cognitive behavioral therapy for people who were depressed, but if there was an extremely severe or complex case no one would have thought to call me to help, and I doubt I would have been comfortable doing so.

It takes time, discipline, and dedication to learn a skill at a level few people achieve, and those who dedicate themselves to this endeavor have a tremendous advantage. There is simply nothing quite like being known as an authority figure to drive business your way.

The idea of building expertise is even more important in today's marketplace precisely because markets have become so diverse and competitive. Consider this example in Figure 5.1.

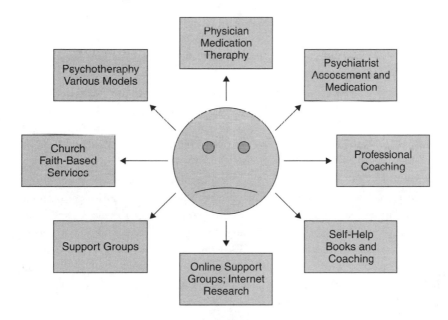

Figure 5.1   Entry Points for Mental Health Treatment

Suppose there's a man out there right now who is in a significant amount of emotional pain. Perhaps he's depressed, and it hasn't lifted in weeks. This person will most likely take some action in an effort to relieve that pain. But in today's marketplace he has a number of options to choose from as an entry point into the mental health system. He can call his primary care physician, who may prescribe antidepressants; he could get help and support through his church; or maybe he's too afraid to talk with someone so he does research on the Internet or goes to a mental health social networking site for support. We could go on and on exploring the possibilities available to him.

Many businesses and individuals struggle in this kind of competitive marketplace, because they have not earned a certain level of credibility in the mind of the consumer. If, for example, a health care professional has no distinguishing characteristics or credentials, then why would someone choose that person when so many options are available?

In order to stay competitive in this kind of marketplace you have to ask yourself this question.

How do you get noticed in the most cluttered marketplace in the history of mankind?

Expertise and authority go a long way toward answering this question.

CHANGE THE WAY YOU WORK IN THE PROFESSION

In 1999, I was just about finished with the mental health profession. I was an eight-year veteran in the field, licensed and managing several programs in Boston. I was newly married and wondering how in the world I was going to grow in this profession that I loved while living in one of the most expensive cities in America.

That was the end of it—too much frustration and not enough opportunity. Until one day, a former colleague and friend shared with me an amazing story about changes he had made in his professional life that ultimately led him to success in the profession. I gained a significant amount of insight from his story, not the least of which was the fact that hard work and dedication would serve me well in my quest to become the very best mental health professional I was capable of being. Rather than expecting things to come to me, rather than passing up opportunities or going through the motions, I decided I'd be the initiator. Rather than being average at a lot of things, I chose to become very good at a few things. I set new goals in this direction and have spent the past several years learning, growing, and taking advantage of new opportunities that came my way. It has made all the difference in terms of my personal enjoyment and the general satisfaction I get from doing my work.

So needless to say, I was pleasantly surprised when I decided to pick up Malcolm Gladwell's book, *Outliers*. One of the compelling arguments he makes in his analysis of success is, in fact, the very argument I began to make and test years ago. In his book, he states that psychologists and neurologists who study performance and expertise, in general, believe that a magic number exists that enables true mastery to exist, and that number is 10,000 hours of practice.

My excitement about this phenomenon, however, lies not in the amount of time required but the idea that shifting your time and energy in new and more productive ways can have such a powerful impact.

Things get even more intriguing when Gladwell chooses to look more closely at groups of people who are gifted and successful in their fields. When you analyze these groups, you begin to see that innate talent plays a smaller and smaller role in distinguishing one person from another. At that level, the factor that plays the biggest role is in fact preparation. He goes on to argue that at some point innate ability has a cutoff point—meaning you need to possess enough ability to be "good enough," and after that, most success comes from the opportunities you are given and, more importantly, what you choose to do with those opportunities.

So for fun, let's assume that a large majority of people who enter the mental health field and successfully complete graduate school do, in fact, possess some level of talent and innate ability as helping professionals. If this were the case, determinants of success would appear to center around your approach to future skill development along with your ability and willingness to take advantage of opportunities available to you.

Gladwell continues his discussion in this area with an examination of the work of a psychologist named K. Anders Ericsson at Berlin's Elite Academy of Music. In the 1990s Dr. Ericsson and his colleagues looked at a group of extremely talented violinists and analyzed these musicians in three groups. Group one were those students with the potential to become world-class violinists. Group two represented those students judged to be "very good" and group three were students who were good but unlikely to ever play professionally.

As they studied the progression of their careers from early age to present day, they found that none of the students were simply naturals, meaning none were musicians who could simply play without any work or effort. They also did not find any students in the three groups who lacked innate ability and simply overcame that deficit through hard work. Their research suggested that once musicians were "good enough" to be admitted to the Berlin academy the only thing that distinguished the three groups was how hard each of them worked. By the age of 20, the students who were the best in their class, the true masters, were practicing significantly more than everyone else. By this age, group three had totaled 4,000 hours of practice time while group two totaled 8,000 hours. And how many practice hours did Group one have by age 20? You guessed it—10,000 hours.

In study after study, Malcolm Gladwell finds this pattern, and he offers some rather interesting examples as proof, from Mozart to the Beatles to Bill Gates.

One of the things I preach to people who are willing to listen is the idea of changing your routine. I call it **"Creating an Exercise Program for Your**

Career," and in many respects it is based on the principles Gladwell defines through the 10,000-hour rule. The idea is simple. Once you have thoroughly examined your interests, passions, and goals, take some time to do an inventory of how you spend your days. Then, make an effort to redefine those days by dedicating more time to things within the field you are passionate about. Instead of spending two hours at night watching baseball or reality TV, use that time to engage in activities that are directly related to your goals. Learn something new by volunteering your time, spend two hours researching a topic of interest to you, or read a book on a special area within mental health. It can be any number of things. If you choose to take this step and are committed to this effort for six months, I promise you will see an incredible difference. At the end of that time period you will be more knowledgeable, more experienced, more motivated, and better positioned in the marketplace than you were six months prior.

I have provided a useful worksheet in the back of this book to help get you going!

BUILD EXPERTISE BY FINDING YOUR MARKET NICHE

My advice, whether you have just entered the field or have spent many years practicing, is to identify an area within the overall market in which you can become a known entity. People often make the mistake of trying to be all things to all people. They become generalists, which creates the perception of mediocrity and positions you right smack in the middle of the marketplace. You run the risk of becoming lost in the crowd of faceless people who are all competing for the same job opportunities and the same prospects. The solution is to become what your competition is not by becoming an expert and/or specialist in one or two smaller segments of the market. Identify areas where there is less competition and position yourself to be at the forefront of that market.

How do you choose your market niche? I suggest identifying what interests you and then thoroughly researching those areas to determine the viability of that particular market. A good place to start would be asking yourself these questions.

- Do I already have a head start in certain sub-specialty areas?
- Do I have a captive audience or group of people who can serve as a foundation for growth within an identified market?
- Is the specialty I am considering specific enough to make me unique, yet large enough to support my efforts?
- How many prospective customers are there for this market niche I have identified?

- What/who are my primary competitors within this specialty?
- What competitive advantages do I currently have?
- What is the timeline in which I can effectively position myself within this market?
- What are the financial growth opportunities for this market?

Many business professionals make the mistake of jumping into a venture without effectively researching the market to determine its viability and how it fits them. Take the time to be strategic in your career planning, and avoid the temptation to skip this step. Here are some helpful research tips to get you started.

- **Professional Associations**: Research mental health associations to learn about major players in the industry, innovative services, and specialties along with training opportunities to begin the process of building knowledge and expertise.
- **Demographic Data**: If you are looking to target and research clients directly, you will need demographic information for your geographical location. A good starting point on the Internet would be: http://www.esri.com/data/esri_data/tapestry.html. You can enter zip codes for your area to generate reports that will include average household income, age, population size, and much more. The service is free and is an excellent tool for researching market segments. The site uses what is called a Tapestry Segmentation System that divides U.S. residential areas into 65 segments based on demographic variables and client behavior characteristics to provide an accurate and detailed description of America's neighborhoods.
- **Census Data**: U.S. Census data can also be a helpful tool and guide. It will provide you with all kinds of information about your geographical area. Go to http://www.census.gov/.
- **Researching Businesses**: Bizstats offers you information about small companies within a particular market segment. They do charge a nominal fee for detailed industry searches but it is worth the money. For example, if you are looking at substance abuse treatment programs, it will allow you to research the average profit margin for that market; and this can help you decide whether or not your specialty market is worth exploring further and who your competition will be. Go to http://www.bizstats.com/.

Effectively identifying smaller segments of the market and building expertise in those areas will take time, dedication, and hard work, however, the rewards are well worth the effort. One of the great secrets of top performing sales professionals is the fact that they are willing to target unique markets and dedicate themselves to becoming experts and leading authorities within those areas. If you move yourself in this direction, you will open the door to much greater possibilities. And along the way, as you grow in the profession and work toward your goals, you will be able to use your expanding knowledge base to build systems and service offerings that will earn you increased credibility, authority, and recognition in the field.

Turn Your Knowledge and Expertise into Value for Clients

Successful sales professionals set up marketing vehicles and systems that offer tremendous value for their customers. This value goes well beyond the scope of their product or service and is perhaps one of the most important lessons to learn as you market yourself and work toward increasing your reputation in the community. Offering free services to potential clients is a great way to build credibility, and there are a variety of ways in which you can accomplish this and begin the process of building a reputation within your target market. Let me give an example to show how adding value can increase your credibility in the eye of the customer.

Several years after finishing graduate school I decided that one of my areas of expertise would be career development for health care professionals with my unique sub-specialty being the effective use and integration of sales and marketing principles to build career growth. My initial approach was to build a training program based on my breadth of knowledge in this area and to offer this training as a free service to specific populations. My initial point of entry was graduate schools and universities in my geographical area. School administrators were more than happy to have me come and present on this topic since I was offering a free service. I delivered the training on a few occasions and provided participants with several different ways to reach me and to become a part of my resource group, where they could receive updates in terms of service offerings, trainings, and events that would help build their careers. Students enjoyed the program and gave positive feedback to administrators, which led to increasing opportunities to present at other universities beyond my local area. This initial 90-minute free training gave significant value to the students who were preparing to enter the marketplace, and as a result, my target market expanded significantly. The overall benefits to me were numerous, and the following are just a few that resulted from this initial step.

- Visibility in my local community and beyond
- Establishment as an expert in a particular niche market
- An opportunity to edit and expand my training programs and workshops by testing content to see what was effective and not so effective

- Growth of my user group so I could market my services to participants both now and in the future

The general take-away from this discussion — choose from a variety of vehicles and techniques that will allow you to reach consumers from a position of authority. Find opportunities to showcase your knowledge and expertise. Your efforts in this regard will begin building your influential power and will help to expand your consumer base.

BECOME PUBLISHED: YOU HAVE UNIQUE OPPORTUNITIES!

Imagine someone in the community who has been feeling depressed for several weeks. He thought his mood would improve over time, but continued to experience many common symptoms associated with depression. This person did not know where to turn for help so he went online and conducted an Internet search by typing in the words "therapist" and "depression". What he found are a few links that identify editorials, press releases, and expert articles written by you! In this instance you have just ended any chance of other mental health practitioners in the community earning that person's business.

You may be thinking, "How do you obtain that kind of publicity? It's extremely difficult to get into a newspaper or have an article published. I don't think it's realistic to think you can accomplish that." I am here to tell you that it can be accomplished, and it is much easier than people would have you believe. The secret lies in understanding the resources available to you and using them to your advantage.

Every day there are television reporters, newspaper writers, and thousands of professionals on the Internet who are starving for new and interesting information they can market to their audiences. If you understand their needs and identify the systems they access, then you can be very successful in providing them with information that will serve to enhance your credibility. In today's world, marketing experts and sales professionals are all aware of a vast array of resources you may not have known existed. Here are a few of those publishing secrets that will get your name out there and help earn you recognition in your industry.

Article Writing

A little over a year ago I was talking to a former college classmate, and he began telling me about some of the work he was doing. During our talk he referenced several articles he had written that were picked up by regional business magazines across the country. He informed me that the publicity he received from some of his articles led to tremendous business opportunities that helped launch his career.

"I never knew you were such an excellent writer," I said. He responded by telling me he wasn't really a great writer. He simply identified a topic he thought was in demand within the marketplace, did a little research, and decided to write about it. "Yeah, but it must have been truly impressive if you were able to get it published and reach such a broad audience." Wrong again! He told me he used one of several online directories that publish articles, and he assumed I had known about these services since everyone in his business knew of them. Sadly, I had no idea what he was talking about, so I decided to do a little research and discovered some incredibly powerful resources.

One of the great things about the Internet today is the amount of marketing opportunities available to you. The Web is so decentralized and has become such a social medium that it holds tremendous power for those who understand its technology. Online article directories are one of those opportunities worth learning more about.

These directories are searched by thousands of people every day who are looking for content for their newsletters, web sites, newspapers, and journals. The better sites typically have a review process where you can submit an article for publication. A team of editors will review your submission and determine whether it is suitable for online publication. Once it is approved you have earned publication status on the World Wide Web! Even better is the fact that these services are typically free of charge and allow you to include your bio. In addition, you can track who has read your article and who has chosen to publish it on their web sites.

When you submit your article in this format, you give viewers permission to use your article for their publications as long as your name and contact information is included. Article marketing such as this ultimately produces a viral effect that is highly valued in the marketing world. Internet users visit these sites in search of interesting content. People who like your article may choose to use it on their web sites or in their newsletters, thereby giving you exposure to totally different audiences. In addition, if someone were to search a specific topic on the Internet that you wrote about, they would find a link identifying you as an "expert author." How are people able to find you on the Internet? Search engines assign rankings to content on the Web, and one of their main ranking criteria is linkages you have with other web sites. The more you are linked throughout the Web the more you are recognized by these tools and the more accessible you become.

Having a presence on the Internet gives you tremendous credibility and leverage. This is extremely important in today's world since most savvy prospects will do research on the Internet before making a purchase decision. They may hear about you and choose to search your name online. What if your name comes up referring to several publications you had written? Better yet, what if links come up where other vendors quote you and your article? It happens all the time and it can happen to you just as easily!

Online publications are great marketing tools, and I would recommend taking advantage of these services as soon as possible. Begin writing today, become published on the Web, and watch your network and credibility grow!

Here are a few online publication resources I have found that will help get you started.

www.ezinearticles.com (my personal favorite)

www.articlecity.com

www.submityourarticle.com

Generate Your Own PR

Public relations is another area of business greatly affected by the rise and expansion of the Internet. In the past, press releases were highly regulated. Gatekeepers could be found everywhere, and you needed the right relationships if you were to generate publicity through the media. But no longer! You don't need public relations firms or strong relationships with reporters and influential media types to get the publicity you seek. All you need is some creativity and the right resources to begin issuing your own releases online.

This method costs money. However, it is worth the investment simply because it can be such a powerful tool for you. One reason why it is so powerful is that press releases you generate online are automatically included in news sections on sites such as Yahoo! and Google. Your press release will be front and center next to the top news stories of the day. Think about it. Do you ever browse these major news sites? What impression would it create for you if a colleague of yours were listed among the major news stories of the day? What would your prospects or potential clients think when they see you listed in that section? Once again, this type of marketing will create a tremendous credibility gap between you and your competition.

On top of all of these benefits, there is the possibility that other news outlets across the country will use your press release. If it is a significant topic and if there is broad enough interest you may find it picked up and used by any number of media outlets—television, print, Internet.

So what do you write about in a press release? A few paragraphs about a topic of interest to you would be a great start. For example, let's say you are a psychotherapist with a specialty in trauma work. You are beginning to treat more and more servicemen and their families as a result of the current political climate. You could talk about statistics related to trauma at home and abroad, talk about the lack of recognition and services to support our troops, and offer some key points of consideration in terms of clinical interventions. You do all this and use your name in the process.

"Trauma Assessment and Intervention Sorely lacking on our Home front."

Ms. X, licensed therapist and trauma counselor, finds that trauma related difficulties are on the rise and families are suffering greatly due to a general lack of awareness and lack of treatment services. . . .

Get the idea? Take a look at some of the press release sites available to you and try it out. Very few people are taking advantage of these resources, and you'll be pleasantly surprised by the results when you do. Here are a few of these services worth looking into.

www.prweb.com (one of the best press release sites on the Internet!)

www.onlinepressreleases.com (another good press release site)

www.falkowinc.com/inc/proactive_report.html (excellent press release newsletter offering up-to-date information and resources)

Write a Book!

So far we've talked about article marketing and online press releases as excellent tools for becoming a recognized expert in your field. These techniques represent steps few people in our industry use to build recognition and authority. The great thing about these techniques is that they serve as a springboard for greater opportunities. For example, you may start by publishing an article online and find the experience worthwhile and enjoyable. As you further identify your niche markets and you immerse yourself in learning and growth around these areas, you'll find that new ideas will come to the forefront. These ideas might lead to the creation of more articles. Later on you might use the skills and techniques identified in these articles to create a series of presentations or workshops that help grow your practice and increase your visibility. Ultimately, this process of becoming an expert creates a snowball effect. Your motivation and focus brings about a growth in knowledge and skill level, which in turn gives you the ability to offer more services.

If you find yourself in this mode, then let me suggest one more logical progression—become an author and write a book. Why not? If you've come this far, then writing a book is not out of the realm of possibility.

I am not necessarily proposing that you write a book, take it to a publisher and have it become a *New York Times* best seller. That may be one possibility, but there are other possibilities available to you. Marketing guru Mark Joyner wrote an e-book called *The Rise of the Author* (http://www.simpleology.com/training/riseoftheauthor) that I highly recommend you read. In it he talks about the unique opportunity available to all of us at this moment in time. The evolution of the World Wide Web as a decentralizing force gives people incredible opportunity and influence if they choose to take action.

E-Books

E-books are a great example of this phenomenon. They are becoming more and more accepted in contemporary society, and as result, more and more quality products are available via e-book.

If you have written several articles about a topic of interest to you, then why not combine these articles into an online book you use as a marketing tool? Being an author of a book, whether it is published by a major outfit or online, will take you to a different level of credibility and respectability within your industry. It will open up opportunities not available to you in the past, such as speaking engagements, consulting projects, or high-level job opportunities.

Creating an e-book is a great first step and once you accomplish this you have several options moving forward. You can offer portions of the book to your prospects and/or user group as a free preview. You can sell the book online and build awareness of your expert status. If it does well and garners attention, a publisher with the means and financial power to produce and market your book on a larger scale may approach you.

My point here is to encourage you to be open to the realm of possibilities. With a little time and effort you can create a book in some way, shape, or form. And, once again, the Internet offers you incredible opportunity! Want to create real impact and take advantage of online e-commerce? You can post your e-book on Amazon.com by simply registering with them! People will be able to search a topic or search your name and find you and your book available for purchase.

Once your e-book is available for purchase there are even more exciting opportunities available. Consider this interesting opportunity: Amazon has a ranking system based on number of books purchased within a set point of time. If you understand their system, you can dedicate your marketing efforts within specific time periods to produce a temporary spike in sales. If you do this effectively, you too can become a best-selling author on Amazon! Marketing expert Mark Joyner studied this process, and at one point in time his book, *The Irresistible Offer*, became the number two bestseller on Amazon. How much credibility does that afford him? How much influence does he have when he is able to make the claim that he is a best-selling author?

The answer is obvious, and it can work for you!

THE ART OF PUBLIC SPEAKING

If you were to ask a group of people at the top of their respective industries to identify the most important and effective skill that helped them achieve success, chances are the majority would list public speaking ability. At its core, public speaking is about the art of persuasion, not presenting information. You are speaking on a specific topic in order to gain audience trust and buy-in; if you do this effectively, you are on the fast track to success and growth in your field.

Public speaking is the most powerful sales and marketing tool you have at your disposal. It builds a tremendous amount of credibility, effectively grows business networks, and offers value to others through knowledge sharing. There is no better way to sell yourself and promote your services! Yes, it takes preparation and effort. Yes, there are many people who fear speaking in front of a group, but you can overcome these fears easily if you follow the other steps we have discussed and identify specialty areas of expertise that you are passionate about. Nothing builds confidence quite like preparation and passion.

If you would like to rise above 95% of all people in your marketplace, begin studying presentation skills and become comfortable as a public speaker. The more opportunities you have to speak and the better you become, the more persuasive and influential you will be.

Section 1: The Do's and Don'ts When Presenting

Although public speaking is an incredibly powerful communication tool, it is also one of the most misused. With that in mind let's examine some incredibly useful techniques that can turn your average everyday presentation into a powerful high impact experience that will leave a lasting impression.

Designing Your Talk

When you are asked to deliver a talk, how do you begin creating the framework for your presentation? I would venture a guess that you begin by turning on the computer to use slide show software such as PowerPoint or Keynote. However, before you begin that phase of development, I recommend you put away the computer and engage in a more creative process that is not limited to or constrained by technology. Going offline gives you far more freedom to identify and define the purpose and structure of your talk.

An obvious starting point when you are looking to build the elements of your presentation is to think about the purpose and goal of your talk. Who is your target audience? What are their needs and wants? What do you hope people leave with once the talk is done? How do you want them to feel? What action(s) do you want them to take? Engaging in a creative process before working on slide development and design will go a long way toward ensuring your talk has clarity of purpose.

Once you have an overall focus and purpose for your presentation, you can begin defining the key elements and structure of your talk. A great way to accomplish this is to visually map things out so you can put your ideas out there and see where they might fit within the context of your overall presentation. There are a number of ways to accomplish this including the use of flip chart paper, white boards, or sticky notes. I prefer the sticky note method because it allows you to visualize various ideas and concepts while giving you the ability to add and rearrange components easily. Figure 5.2 offers you an example from one of my brainstorming efforts.

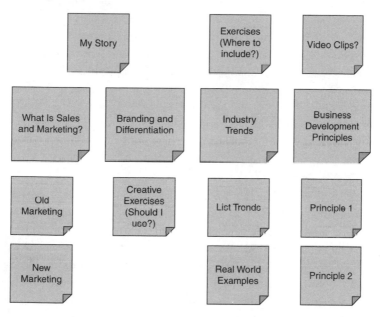

Figure 5.2 *Snapshot of a Brainstorming Session*

In the initial stages I use sticky notes as a free association exercise where I write down all the ideas I initially have for a particular workshop. I don't use any filters during this process. Whatever comes to mind gets written on a sticky note, no matter how absurd or irrelevant it may seem. I place the sticky notes on a wall in no particular order and this, in turn, helps me to see the big picture. Patterns and themes begin to identify themselves, which brings about new ideas that I add to the wall in the form of new sticky notes. From this exercise I am able to identify many of the main topics for my presentation. In the example shown in Figure 5.2, I initially identified four core elements for my workshop, which are identified as larger sticky notes. Once I have an idea of what the foundation elements for my talk are, I can slowly build content around each of these elements by moving notes under each of the categories. If there are new ideas or questions I have while going through this process, I place them above the core elements as placeholders so I might eventually find a place for each. This is a great exercise to conduct before you begin creating presentation slides.

Starting Your Presentation

Too many presentations lose people right off the bat for a variety of reasons, but perhaps the most important one has to do with the introduction. The beginning of your presentation sets the tone immediately; and if you lose the audience right from the start, then you have a tough road ahead of you.

Have you ever watched *American Idol*? Most people who watch the show say they know on the very first note whether the person singing is going to have a great or not so great performance. That first note is felt immediately, and if it is experienced positively, it creates a memorable experience for the audience. The same holds true when we talk about giving a presentation. The next time you attend a presentation, listen for the first few words, pay attention to your initial impression, and see if that has any bearing as to the overall quality and value you associate with the entire experience.

Transferable Concepts

One of the best ways to create a powerful first impression is to approach the beginning in a less traditional manner. A great way to accomplish this is through the use of story. It does not have to be a personal story. Any compelling story related to your topic will do. The first thing that a good story does is identify a theme or common experience that serves as a **transferable concept** for the participant. By this I mean that audience members can relate to the story and will be able to identify their own personal experiences as you go through your presentation. Adopting this model allows you to connect with people on an emotional level.

I often give career development workshops to university students. When I do so, I begin with an amusing story about my own experiences coming out of college and/or graduate school. Why? First and foremost the story contains powerful lessons learned that I will emphasize later on in the workshop. The second reason is that audience members will be able to relate to my experience and will search for a like-minded story from their own personal history. When doing this, people are able to see the linkages and commonalities between my story and theirs. This helps build immediate rapport and quickly engages the participants because they now see how the information presented will be directly related to their needs.

Surprise the Audience by Avoiding the Predictable

I would also suggest taking the story theme even further and making an effort to begin your presentation as if you were in the middle of your speech. Avoid going through the basic introductions, agenda, and overview of what you hope to accomplish. If you feel this is a must, then have someone else do that part for you. When you get up to begin your talk, pause for a brief moment and then launch into your story.

Tip: Don't tell the audience you are going to begin by telling a story. Simply begin your talk with the story itself.

Be passionate, intriguing, and powerful as you tell the story. This surprise compels the audience to listen as they will be intrigued by your approach and will make a concerted effort to understand how your story will fit into the greater whole of the presentation.

Ask a Good Question

A great alternative to telling a story is beginning your presentation with a powerful and thought-provoking question. Once again, I recommend avoiding the traditional introduction. When I use this approach, I try not to telegraph my beginning by telling the audience what I will be doing. I use the element of surprise to quickly gain interest and buy-in from the audience.

I have used this technique quite effectively with some of my graduate school career workshops. This particular question tends to elicit strong emotional responses from the audience:

"How many of you right now find yourselves constantly thinking about how you are going to realistically make a living as mental health professionals?"

Once I ask this question I remain silent for a period of time. Sometimes people are compelled to respond, and a dialogue begins. At other times the room stays quiet. Either way I have created a shift in energy within the room by asking a blunt and honest question that everyone can relate to on a personal level. My next step is to follow up this question with some compelling statements that communicate hope and encouragement. After all, the main goal of my workshop is to teach people how to build wealth and success as mental health professionals, and the information I offer will be invaluable to the audience, because it contains information that is proven to improve career growth and success in the field! I am not shy or subtle about my claim. When you are presenting to an audience, be clear and very direct about the value of your expertise.

What Should You Provide to the Audience?

When it comes to handout materials for a presentation, avoid the temptation to provide printed copies of your slide show. Why? For starters, you will be tempted to pack your slides full of detailed information since your intent is to create a leave behind document that people will understand. Unfortunately, this is poor slide design, and it will negatively impact your talk. In addition, sharing your presentation in handout form will distract the audience. They will inevitably leaf through the document during your talk and miss what you have to say. Avoid making this mistake if at all possible.

If you're concerned that people will leave your talk wanting more information, then consider this a good sign. It's good practice to leave your audience wanting more. When your talk is over, offer them opportunities to obtain additional information. You might invite them to e-mail you with questions, suggest they sign up to receive information from your blog, offer them your consulting services, or promote a more comprehensive workshop/seminar that will help answer their questions.

Having said all this, there are still things you can provide to the audience that will create a positive impression. A great leave-behind for your audience is a well-designed and detailed report that clarifies and reinforces the key points made in your presentation. It may include important articles, detailed graphs, and/or charts, worksheets, research studies that support your presentation arguments, and even a resource list. This process may take some additional work on your part, but it will make you memorable and will serve as a great marketing tool.

Other Important Tips

There are many other important skills and useful tips that will help fine-tune your public speaking skills. Below are some of the ones I find most useful.

Present new ideas, not just new information

- Offering useful information is one thing, offering new ideas that participants never thought of before is a whole different ballgame! I attended a sales workshop not long ago, and I left incredibly motivated to change some of the ways I went about doing my business. I was inspired because the presenter offered new ways of approaching my day-to-day activities that I had not thought of before. It opened up new areas for growth.
- Try to identify two to three new concepts and ideas that you will feature in your presentation. Your audience will buy you and your message if you are able to do so.

The primary goal of a presentation should not be information sharing

- If you're looking to become a great presenter you must understand that your ability to connect with the audience on an emotional level is the key to success.

- The transfer of information (e.g., facts, methods) is secondary. People will hear your message on a deeper level and be more inclined to action if you reach them on an emotional level.
- Take a moment to recall the best presentations you have heard during your career. Did you relate to their message on an emotional level? If so, why?

Present exciting and new material that people can apply in their lives

- This is really a spin-off from the first tip, but it takes it a step farther. Be careful about offering new ideas that are great from a theoretical standpoint but virtually impossible to apply in the real world.
- Generate ideas and concepts that people can relate to easily, so they begin telling themselves, "That's a great idea, I can apply that to my line of work immediately and it will yield some powerful results. I'm going to give it a try."
- Inspire action in people by communicating ideas that are transferable and real.

Stick to your plan: Control the flow

- It is easy to get sidetracked when audience members ask questions. When a question is asked that is not quite on task, politely inform the audience that you will answer that specific question at the end of the presentation.
- Why dismiss good questions? It is important to stick to your plan and structure. You are not dismissing questions, rather you are saving them for a more appropriate time.

Don't demand audience participation

- Ugh. Nothing makes my blood boil more than the overuse of audience participation. Okay, I understand that people have good intentions when they take this approach. They want to engage the audience and keep them engaged by asking them to participate. However, be careful when you take this approach. Too many questions or attempts to have the audience participate can become patronizing and annoying.
- Some of my pet peeves in this area:
  - Consistently asking obvious questions to which everyone knows the answers. Of course no one is answering you. The answers are obvious!
  - Saying hello to the audience and then pausing because you are waiting for an enthusiastic hello back. Don't patronize people!

Section 2: Slide Show Design

The PowerPoint Dilemma

PowerPoint has become a critical and essential part of any public speaking opportunity. I've used PowerPoint in a number of different capacities and, for a brief period of time, I considered myself to be somewhat of an expert. Allow me to show you one of my masterpieces.

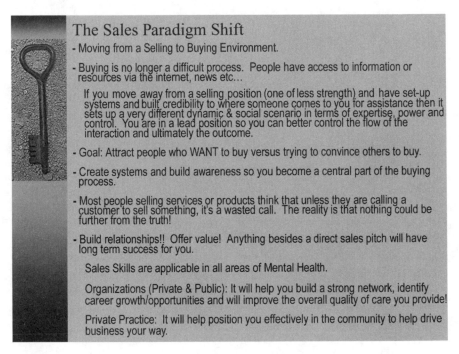

Figure 5.3 *Poor Slide Design Example*

Sadly, as you can see in Figure 5.3, these slides were painful to view and rarely engaged the audience. In an effort to ensure all my ideas were captured I would write long sentences and paragraphs as if I were writing a research paper. In addition to the information I packed into these slides, I also took full advantage of all the bells and whistles PowerPoint offered—the use of sound, text sliding in and out, and clip art images posted wherever I had space. What did this accomplish? Not much other than boring my audience to death. My point is that these mistakes and mishaps are not out of the ordinary. Most PowerPoint presentations today are dreadful but can be easily remedied in a short period of time.

True success with PowerPoint has to do with balancing knowledge sharing with the emotional needs, reactions, and responses of your audience. When you are giving a presentation you are playing to the needs and wants of your audience. You are, in fact, selling ideas and concepts, and this requires an ability to engage others.

Now let's see how PowerPoint can be effectively used. Recently, I coordinated a workshop on neuropsychiatry and neuroscience. Neuroscience is not exactly a light topic, especially for a two-day workshop. I knew that the subject matter could potentially be a tough sell for participants depending on the public speaking skills of the psychiatrist who was giving the talk. He could have easily launched into statistics and a detailed analysis and explanation of biology and chemistry that would have put the audience to sleep no matter how insightful the information. So imagine my pleasant surprise when he began the workshop with a slide of a famous French painting of a nude woman in a park surrounded by several men. With much lighthearted humor, he asked the audience what in the world this women was doing prancing around with no clothes. He used this as a starting point for his neuroscience model. He did this by looking at human behavior (in this case, the nude woman) and then took the audience deeper and deeper until he came to the cellular and chemical levels that were ultimately driving this woman's peculiar behavior.

As the presentation went on, he incorporated a wide variety of images and video clips you would not expect from a talk on neuropsychiatry. He used video clips of his dog to discuss the neuroscience behind behavior and motivation; he showed images and clips of important research studies with lab rats and tragic stories of people who had suffered severe brain damage. All these things supported his explanation of a detailed and sophisticated neuroscience model. This is a great example of just how effective and powerful slides can be when used appropriately.

Let's look more closely at some PowerPoint slides that are significantly more powerful and effective than the work I previously presented. As an example, let's say you work for a family treatment center specializing in child abuse cases. You are looking for donations from the community and funding from state agencies. You might try using a slide such as the one shown in Figure 5.4 and make it the foundation for talking about what you offer.

Or perhaps you are giving a talk on the problem of homelessness in your community in an attempt to foster support for increased housing and hospital programs for the mentally ill. Instead of giving a list of statistics or a long list of detailed bullet points you might try something like the image shown in Figure 5.5.

The use of images is an excellent way to communicate emotion that can emphasize the importance of your proposed initiatives and interventions. As your audience responds to the power of the image or images, you can reinforce your ideas through the power of a story.

Figure 5.4   *Good Slide Design: Sample 1*

Figure 5.5   *Good Slide Design: Sample 2*

Slideshow Design Principles that Say "Wow"
Someone once told me that design is a medium for persuasion, not decoration.
I never truly understood this statement nor did I incorporate it into the slides
I created until recently.

Here are some important slide design principles that can have a huge impact on your ability to deliver a fantastic presentation as a mental health professional. The slide images I've included come from talks I've given over the years. Hopefully, you'll see a positive progression in my slide development based on the successful adoption of the following design principles.

Signal to Noise Ratio

This design principle looks at the ratio of relevant (Signal) to irrelevant (Noise) elements on a slide. The higher the signal to noise ratio the better. If you achieve a good level of simplicity in your design you are in essence improving your ability to convey a message to your audience.

In addition, the use of empty space is another important factor when looking at this ratio. Contrary to popular belief, empty space has a purpose. It gives a voice to the positive elements already in the slide. It helps to build recognition where you have very little time to create an impression.

Figures 5.6 and 5.7 provide examples.

Old Objectives Slide

- In this slide I used a lot of bullet points in order to get my message across. There is too much text, making it difficult to read.
- The use of clip art is a distraction and has no purpose.

Objectives

- Build awareness of the scope and severity of the problem of suicide in children and adolecents.
- Suicide Fact vs. Myth. Explore the realities of teen suicide in our culture.
- Discuss and review the warning signs.
- Recognize certain issues that increase the at-risk factor in a youth.
- Discuss steps you can take when warning signs are exhibited.
- Review a suicide awareness and assessment model.
- Discuss teen suicide scenarios.
- Conduct a group discussion on factors that place youth ar risk.
- Learn about community resources that can help in dealing with a possible suicidal situation.

Figure 5.6 *Old Objectives Slide*

New Objectives Slide

- I decided to update my objective slide by reducing the noise created when I chose to use too much text. I hoped to gain better clarity of message through a more elegant design that leveraged more empty space.

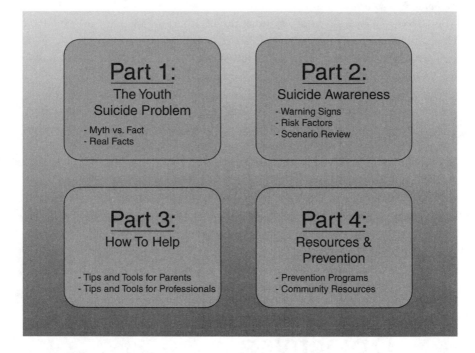

Figure 5.7   *New Objectives Slide*

Slide Balance and The Rule of Thirds

Slide balance involves a number of important design rules. You can produce a more dynamic and engaging feel when it is used to its utmost potential. Figure 5.8 is one example of poor use of balance.

Old Exercise Slide

There is very little in this slide that would engage viewers. Because it is a boring and standard design, it does little to draw a readers' attention to the main points I am trying to make. I essentially created a cookie cutter chart that may have been more confusing and distracting than impactful.

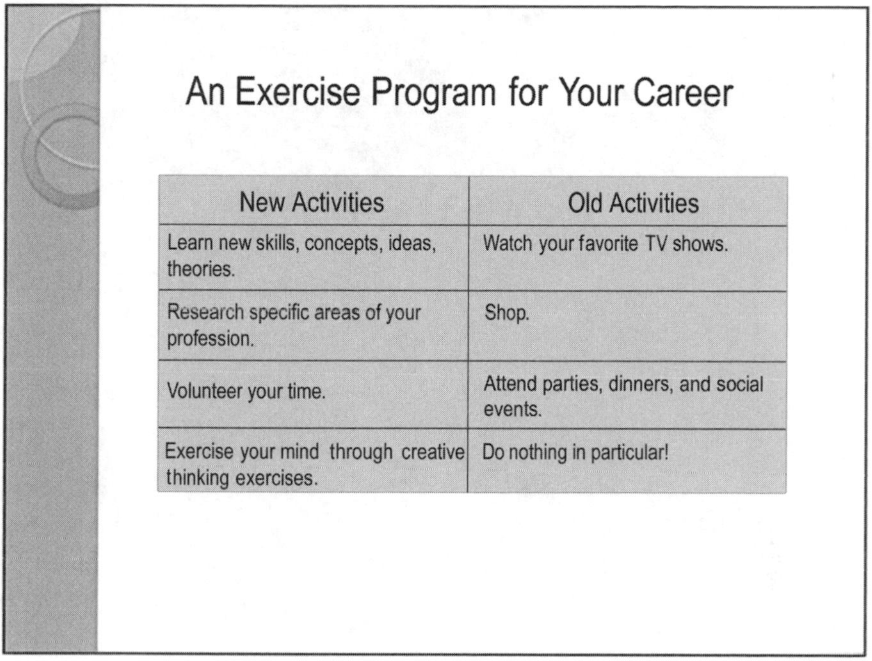

An Exercise Program for Your Career

New Activities	Old Activities
Learn new skills, concepts, ideas, theories.	Watch your favorite TV shows.
Research specific areas of your profession.	Shop.
Volunteer your time.	Attend parties, dinners, and social events.
Exercise your mind through creative thinking exercises.	Do nothing in particular!

Figure 5.8   *Old Exercise Slide*

New Exercise Slide and The Rule of Thirds

A good idea when using text with images is to place the text within a larger image. This helps to create a cleaner and more balanced slide. I also used empty space to create more impact.

And finally, I used an interesting rule called the rule of thirds. This is a basic design technique that helps to add balance and higher aesthetic quality to your slides. If you divide the slide into nine sections as indicated in Figure 5.9 you will have four intersecting lines. These four intersecting points are areas where you might want to consider placing your key images versus placing them in the center. It creates a far more interesting and engaging slide!

There are many more tips to explore when it comes to slide design but the concepts I have just discussed should help improve your slide development significantly.

Figure 5.9   New Exercise Slide and the Rule of Thirds

Practical Slideshow Review

As a brief review, here's a summary of some of the tips and techniques we discussed that you should consider the next time you are working on a slide presentation.

1. Limit the amount of text you use on your slides.
   - Some experts suggest no more than two to three words per bullet point. Others suggest limiting the number of words on a slide to ten.
   - The main message here is to avoid using slides as a documentation tool or as a way for you to explain your message through words. The words you use on a slide should serve as cues that complement the real content, which comes from you.
2. Try to focus on one concept per slide.
3. Use slides that tell a story rather than relate a fact.
4. Use images whenever possible.
   - Substitute images and video clips for words whenever possible.
   - Images are far more powerful and engaging.
5. Practical matters:

- Avoid distracting technical bells and whistles like moving text or fancy slide transitions.
- If a slide appears wordy or confusing, make additional slides to accommodate your ideas and content.
- If you are struggling over a slide that you want to make work, but it just does not seem to fit; it is most likely not worth including in your presentation.
- Avoid using clip art of any kind if possible. Generic clip art looks amateurish. Unique cartoons and powerful images are great, but basic clip art will bring down the look and feel of your slide show.
- Use a white background. Avoid using fancy and overdone backgrounds that take away from the presentation.
- Use a basic font that is clear and easy to read.

SUMMARY

- The Milgram studies (1963) offer insight into the role authority and credibility play in the sales process. Research findings reveal a "deep-seated sense of duty to authority within us all."
- There are few things in the world of business that will get you clients and beat out your competition more than being recognized as an expert in your field.
- Finding your specific market niche is an important step in building credibility. Find a specific market where you can become known, and avoid the trap of trying to be all things to all people.
- At some point innate ability has a cutoff point, meaning you need to posses enough ability to be "good enough," and after that, most of success comes from the opportunities you are given and, more importantly, what you choose to do with those opportunities. Make an effort to restructure how you use your time.
- Create marketing vehicles and systems that offer tremendous value for consumers and keep you highly visible.
- Build credibility by becoming published. In today's age of the Internet there are numerous ways to publish articles, issue press releases, and author books. Review this chapter to learn about some great resources that will get you started.
- When creating a presentation, take creative time away from your computer to generate ideas and to build a solid framework for your talk.
- Create memorable presentations by using slides that support your speech. Use stories and thought provoking questions to engage the audience. Get participants to relate your talk to their own unique world.

- When creating slides, remember that simple and well-balanced designs always win out. Be sure to use the signal to noise ratio and rule of thirds concepts in your designs.
- Avoid the temptation to give your slides to the audience. Offer an online community forum or present them with a comprehensive and well-designed report at the end of the talk. Both options will leave a lasting impression!

CHAPTER SIX

Understanding Buying Motives in Behavioral Health Care

Many of us in the mental health profession have had an experience or two when we made a significant effort to develop and offer a unique clinical service we thought would be an instant success. Unfortunately, most of us have also experienced the frustration of discovering that there was little demand for the service in spite of people's initial feedback and encouragement. And no matter how much more effort and time was spent marketing the service, it still produced very few positive results. In this chapter we take a closer look at this problem by exploring the psychology behind human motivation and the buying phenomenon.

The frustration experience I reference in the preceding paragraph is quite broad in its scope. It can be and is experienced at all levels within the mental health profession. Some examples of what I am referring to are as follows:

- An eating disorder clinic of some prominence is forced to close its doors due to increasing costs and a shrinking consumer base. Its closing brings about complaints from members of the community arguing the need for these services.
- A state mental health agency is overrun with mental health problems in the community with little to no support from the state government. The result—a rise in violence, an increase in homelessness, and limited support resources for those in need. These negative events do little to motivate state representatives to act.
- A therapist responds to years of community feedback asking for a substance abuse education program for adolescents. He opens his doors for six months but is unable to sustain a census beyond three to four people and ends up closing the program.

One of the common themes within these and other scenarios is the perceived and expressed need of these services without the call to action that motivates prospects to use or sign off on these services. There becomes a definite distinction between wanting a service and using a service. This phenomenon is the primary focus of this chapter.

It is an important topic to discuss, because we are dealing with subtle differences that, if understood more fully, will help you to make more accurate decisions when choosing to go to market with your product or service. Always remember, the client's reasons for buying are far more important than the actual process of selling your services. Whether these reasons are logical makes no difference when looking at sales success factors.

TRIGGER POINTS IN MENTAL HEALTH

I was first introduced to the phrase *trigger point* during a conversation with a successful sales professional as part of my research for this book. His introduction of this concept gave me great insight into some of the reasons why he was so successful in his industry. Very little is known about trigger points in the mental health profession, and yet the concept is incredibly important for understanding the buying phenomenon.

In essence, trigger points are events that *create an essential need* for a person or group of people. When we apply this to a business development model, we see that trigger points are the stimulus behind any buying decision and/or action that moves someone toward a buying decision.

And here is the most important point with regard to this phenomenon: If people experience a trigger event, *they will always act. They will always seek help.*

Once this kind of event takes place the only real question becomes, who will they seek help from. Recognizing, anticipating, and understanding trigger points in people will help you position yourself so they choose to seek help from you.

Examples

Let's look at some examples to help clarify what we mean by trigger points and then discuss their overall utility in the mental health profession.

A common business example illustrates the presence and absence of buying motives. I enjoy Best Buy, so let's look at a couple of scenarios that might occur at their store. In this first example a woman goes to her local Best Buy in search of a new computer. She has a perfectly fine computer at home but fancies herself to be a tech junkie, so she is always keeping an eye on new trends in the marketplace. She tells the salesman she is looking for the latest and greatest computers currently on the market. The salesperson chooses to spend a significant amount of time chatting with her about the best computer systems Best Buy has to offer. He enjoys her energy level and interest. An hour passes, and she thanks the salesman for his time and leaves the store empty-handed. In this scenario, there is no trigger event, no pressing need for this woman to purchase a new computer, because she already owns one that allows her to do most of what she wants.

Now let's look at a different scenario. In this example, a father and son come to the store looking for a computer; the father wants to make sure his son has the necessary resources to be successful when he goes off to college in a few weeks. This is the trigger event, and it should signal to the salesperson that the only question now is whether or not the father will purchase a computer from him.

The salesman who recognizes which prospect will have the highest probability of delivering a sale (the woman looking for the best technology or the father/son duo) will be the one with the most sales success at the end of the day. Why? He will be more targeted in his sales approach and will essentially qualify prospects more effectively in order to determine where he should spend the majority of his time.

What about the Mental Health Profession?

Let's consider a family struggling with a child who is demonstrating increasingly bizarre and dangerous behaviors. Not an uncommon scenario in our line of work. Let's also say that the problem behaviors have escalated to the point where no one is safe in the home. When this unfortunate scenario becomes a reality, it serves as a trigger event for the family to seek out mental health services. It may be unclear what will best meet the needs of the family, but they will no doubt be seeking and using some type of mental health service. A mental health professional who successfully speaks to this trigger point, whether it is in an advertisement or through some other communication vehicle, will be the one most likely to be given the opportunity to provide services for the child and family.

Now let's look at another scenario and see how it might be different and why.

A father contacts a therapist with questions about his 17-year-old son as his son has run into some trouble at school. School counselors and administrators have noticed a change in the young man's behavior, which includes skipping class, angry outbursts, and suspected use of alcohol. The school spoke with both parents and gave them the therapist's contact information as a referral source. They suggested the family seek counseling services for their son. The therapist, during the initial phone call, makes an effort to answer some of the father's questions, and they schedule a family session. On the day of the session the family does not show, and they do not return the therapist's follow-up phone calls. In this scenario there really is no true trigger point from the family's perspective. As a clinician, you may believe that the young man's problems suggest a definite need for clinical intervention, but the family obviously does not view it as that critical a situation. They were ambivalent from the start and most likely contacted the therapist to appease the school. Whatever the rationale behind their decision, it is clear that they perceived no current pressing need that would motivate them to seek out and use counseling services.

This latter scenario speaks to one of the main challenges mental health professionals face on a daily basis: breaking through denial systems that prevent people from seeking appropriate treatment. Someone who understood buyer motivation principles might have been skilled enough during the initial conversation with the father to elicit an appropriate trigger response so the father would have been able to recognize the severity of the problem and the importance of seeking help for his son.

The proper application of the trigger point concept will help produce positive results for you. In essence, there are two main components or uses for trigger points that are directly applicable to your work situation. They are as follows:

1. **A Market Research Tool**
   - Trigger points help you to recognize and focus your resources only on situations where essential need is present, thereby improving your ability to generate business.
   - Trigger points are an effective prospecting tool. They give you the ability to work more efficiently and to be more targeted in your outreach efforts. They offer a system for qualifying consumers so you can choose what population to focus your business development efforts on.
   - Trigger points serve as a barometer to help you decide whether to offer a service and to better understand where consumer need is most pressing and most important.
   - In larger organizations, an analysis of trigger points can help you determine overall marketing campaigns and business relationships/partnerships to seek out.
   - In private practices, trigger points can help you define your market niche.

2. **A Way to Bring About Hidden Buyer Motivation**
   - Trigger points give you the ability to speak directly to the pressing needs and hidden concerns of consumers.
   - Your awareness of automated response systems resulting from specific trigger events can help you move people along the buying process continuum.

- Eliciting behavioral responses by uncovering trigger events is not about manipulating people to do something they don't want, rather it is about freeing people up and giving them permission to access things that are of important value to them and their well-being. It is about finding the emotional triggers that speak to people and giving them permission to act. The father-son example is a good one to explore. Can you identify the trigger stimuli that will resonate with the father so the child can get the help he needs?

Both of these components speak to the power of trigger points once you understand how to incorporate them into your professional practice. Are you looking to increase your chances for success in whatever services you choose to offer? Do you want to work smarter and be more productive with your time? Understand and explore the presence of trigger events, qualify your prospects, recognize the behavioral cues that lead to buying decisions, and use this knowledge when conducting your day-to-day business.

LESSONS IN BEHAVIORAL PSYCHOLOGY: ACCESSING TRIGGER POINTS IN YOUR MARKETING MESSAGES

While essential need is the hallmark of the trigger point phenomenon, there is an interesting twist to this story that leads us even further into the realm of behavioral psychology. It is here that we recognize the power of **automated response systems** and the critical role played by the existence of specific environmental stimuli. Skilled marketers are highly attuned to these phenomena. Why? Because they use this knowledge to create powerful marketing messages that cue powerful emotional responses they hope will increase buyer motivation. Once you are aware of the presence of trigger points, and you understand the environmental cues that release these triggers, you are doing a much better job of reaching out to your consumer base.

In the hands of unethical professionals this knowledge and these skills can be manipulative and deceitful. However, in the hands of others, they can be used to identify the correct message and the right communication vehicles that will resonate with potential buyers. It is for this reason that I believe we should take a look at the research done in this area. It may help you identify better ways to empower and motivate people so they will choose to use those services that will help them in the long run.

Research Findings

In research psychology circles there are numerous studies identifying fixed action patterns in animals. There is, of course, the famous Pavlovian principle, but there are also a wide variety of clinical research studies exploring behavior sequences in animals. In these studies an animal goes through a series of behaviors depending on the stimulus that is introduced. Researchers have found that once you have isolated the trigger event you can substitute it with something contrived and still bring about the same response pattern. A classic example is the research done with mother turkeys and their maternal instincts. If a chick makes the appropriate "cheep" sound, its mother will care for it. This is the key trigger event. If that specific sound is not present, the mother will kill the chick. Reliance on this stimulus is so entrenched that researchers can introduce seemingly ridiculous substitutes for a baby chick (even stuffed animals portraying natural enemies); and if these substitutes contain a tape recorder playing the required "cheep" sound, then the turkey will care for the object as if it were its own.

What does this research have to do with our examination of human behavior? For starters, it demonstrates the existence of preprogrammed response systems that can be triggered at seemingly inappropriate times if someone understands the trigger event. Human beings also possess these automated response systems. They are, in fact, quite prevalent in much of our day-to-day activity. One reason why these automated response sets exist has to do with living in a highly complex and sophisticated world containing mass amounts of information. In order to thrive in this environment we must adopt principles to help us classify, organize, and process much of the information we encounter. In most instances the response sets we create are highly effective, accurate, and beneficial. They allow us to make quick decisions and to be more efficient with our time.

Following are some examples of response sets or principles we commonly adopt:

- **Higher Price = Better Quality**

    How often do we associate high price with quality? Fairly often. In most cases it is an automatic association. Retailers have been known to take advantage of this principle by overpricing merchandise that has been difficult to sell. The price increase often gives the impression of added value to the consumer, which in turn increases sales.

- **Specific Education/Degree or Title = Expertise/Authority/Credibility**

    We have already discussed the importance of taking advantage of this principle by taking steps to build genuine credibility. This credibility increases your power as a mental health professional.

- **Professional/High Quality Advertisements = Good services and/or products**

    Right or wrong, the look, feel, and delivery of an advertisement leave a lasting impression. If a viewer feels the advertisement is well done, they are more likely to perceive the service or product in a favorable light.

Breaking Through Resistance: Implications for Automated Response Sets

I cannot stress enough the value you receive by simply being more aware of trigger events and automated response patterns. Powerful marketing entities craft their messages with behavioral cues in mind. They understand that people can respond to specific environmental cues in unique ways, however, they are also well aware of general principles and stereotypes adopted by the majority that bring about common behavioral response patterns.

If, for instance, you receive something in the mail that you have learned to associate with being an advertisement, you may be cued to toss the piece of paper in the trash without ever looking at it. There are numerous cues that trigger skepticism and resistance in people. In many industries it is so easy for a consumer to turn you off that it becomes essential for you to study and understand the way a cynical consumer population acts and reacts in order to shape a strategy that will penetrate the skeptical defenses.

The key is to remove the cues that trigger automated response patterns and keep your prospects from immediately putting up their defenses. Once you have lowered the resistance factor and defenses are down, then you make an effort to communicate enough valuable information to build both curiosity and credibility.

PROSPECTING: HOW TO SELL YOUR SERVICES TO THE RIGHT PEOPLE

The ability to sell your services is the lifeblood of any organization and any working individual. One of the biggest stumbling blocks in sales is the process of trying to find someone to sell your services to. Uncovering the proper client base is hard work. It is a process that will cause you to experience considerable challenges and frustration. Too often people are not up to the challenge, and as a result, they begin to cut corners when looking for clients, or they quit the process outright.

Many people start off with good intentions and a sound plan only to lose steam when their efforts are not immediately rewarded. The result is often a lackluster approach in which ineffective sales strategies like cold calling or paying for lead lists become the norm. Unfortunately, these approaches end up being counterproductive. They continue to build frustration, because they are largely ineffective. This has to do with the fact that these approaches cause you to reach out to an audience without making the effort to identify your valid prospects. In essence, you cast your line into a vast ocean with little to no understanding of what lurks beneath.

Prospecting is a common sales term used to define a process for identifying potential clients. And exploring this process is where we will uncover solutions to the challenges we all face when trying to find a proper audience. Developing a prospecting system that reaches out to a specific set of clients with needs and resources that match your service offering represents a big step in the right direction. It begins with an understanding of referral entities and where they fall on a sales continuum.

In my line of business I am approached by all kinds of salespeople trying to persuade me to spend advertising dollars. One day I met with someone about advertising space in our local area malls. "Your message will be in front of well over 100,000 prospects every three months based on our data," he said. Really? Am I really reaching out to 100,000 prospects? Nothing could be further from the truth and this is a common mistake people make time and time again. Most people believe they have a good understanding of their market when they have a list of names, phone numbers, and addresses. Even worse, they'll tell others they have a long list of prospects or they will say they have done their research, and the population size of a specific area gives them access to "over 10,000 prospects." In this case, the salesperson was telling me I had access to 100,000 prospects. The mistake here is being fooled into thinking that these are in fact "prospects" in the truest sense of the word. We misunderstand what a true prospect really is, and this has implications in terms of just how effective our sales efforts can be.

There are four industry standard groupings that sales and marketing professionals use to identify potential consumers. These groupings are very helpful for improving sales conversion rates.

Group 1: The "All" Category

This is the group people are drawing from when they cast their line into a vast ocean or when they tell you there are over 100,000 prospects within their market. In this group there are no exclusionary criteria used. You see this group at face value. It is all encompassing and all-inclusive.

Research suggests that less than 10% of referrals in this category lead to a sale.

Group 2: The "Potential" Category

In this group you use some basic criteria to begin defining a potential group of people you believe might be able to benefit from what you are offering. In this group you might look at age, gender, income level, geographic location, family structure, line of business, and the like. You have eliminated those people who would have no use for your services and have identified a smaller group of people who might be interested in your service or product.

In this category you have a 15% chance of getting a sale from a referral.

Group 3: The "Prospect" Category

In this group you have identified people you know can use your product versus those who might simply be interested. This sometimes occurs when a client gives you the name of an individual or organization they know will benefit from your service. Other times you identify true prospects by talking to them and finding out whether they have a need you can help them fulfill. Regardless how you come about this information, you have narrowed the field once again by identifying people you know can use your service and will benefit from it.

Once again the percentages for making a sale increase. Within this category, your chances of closing a sale are about 35% to 40%.

Group 4: The "Qualified Customer" Category

This final group includes those people who not only *can* use your services but also have the *resources* and *means* to use these services. It is here that you determine whether they have the financial resources necessary, whether they have a pressing need to acquire your service, and whether they see value in what you are offering.

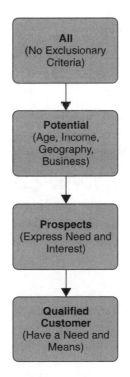

Figure 6.1 The Customer Continuum

Your chances of obtaining a sale within this group are often over 60%!

The further down the line a referral is on this continuum, the more likely you are to make a sale. Why is this so important? The primary reason is that only a certain percentage of people in the marketplace are actually ready and willing clients. The key is to find out who those clients are and avoid spending time and effort selling to those who will never buy from you.

Find the client with the pressing need and develop lead generation systems that will target people at higher levels along the prospect continuum and you will find success.

SUMMARY

- A trigger point is an event that creates an essential need for a person or group of people. Trigger points are the stimulus behind any buying decision and/or action that moves someone toward a buying decision.
- If people are experiencing a trigger event, they will always seek assistance. The only real question is, whom will they choose to help them?
- There are two main uses for trigger points in the mental health profession: (1) a market research tool enabling you to prospect for appropriate clients; (2) uncovering hidden buyer motivation by speaking directly to the needs and wants of potential consumers.
- You can use awareness of preprogrammed automated response sets and take appropriate steps to remove or diffuse them. Your ability to do so will help reduce common defensive reactions that present obstacles for selling services.
- Prospecting is a term used to define a process for identifying potential customers.
- There are four main levels when we talk about consumers. The four levels are defined as follows: (1) The "All" Category; (2) The "Potential" Category; (3) The "Prospect" Category; (4) The "Qualified Customer" Category. The higher the level of the consumer the better chance you have of obtaining a sale.

CHAPTER SEVEN

Sales and Marketing for Mental Health Organizations

Many of my readers work within a larger behavioral health care system where success and survival depends on many factors:

- The service volume provided
- The number of billable hours obtained
- The production of measurable results such as reduction in family violence based on your clinical interventions, improvement in school success, or increased productivity of employees, to name a few

The principles presented throughout this book help contribute to your individual success, but they also directly apply to the collective goals of an organization regardless of the business model. This means they apply equally to a private for-profit business, a non-profit community organization, a large state agency, or any other behavioral health care business entity.

This chapter offers a few additional pieces of information specifically geared toward success factors for behavioral health care organizations.

BUILDING SUCCESSFUL PARTNERSHIPS

Earning business requires understanding the needs of the organization or individuals you are targeting. It is essential to your success, whether you are applying for a grant, responding to a request for proposal, or looking to form a strategic partnership. What follows is a partnership model that can help you earn more business by better understanding the needs of the companies you wish to serve.

Using a Business Motivation Model

Success and growth for behavioral health companies involves the establishment of strong partnerships with other businesses in the community. An example would be a private mental health organization that must establish contracts with state agencies that are looking for community-based services for their clients, or a psychiatric hospital that builds relationships with other hospitals and emergency rooms in the community as a major source of business. A critical factor for winning contract bids and becoming a provider of choice is the ability to understand the business motives and profit model of your prospects. In short, it requires use of a model that gets to the heart of a business leader's mission and overarching goal. That goal is profit, which can be defined in many unique and interesting ways.

Let's look at a real life example as a point of discussion and clarification. Several years ago an organization offering residential services was looking to expand their presence in the marketplace in order to increase call volume, improve their payer mix, and improve admission rates. The company had a high quality clinical model and a proven track record of success. Their intake process, however, was lengthy, cumbersome, and highly selective by design. They viewed this as essential to maintaining the best care possible, as quality was to be their differentiating factor in the marketplace.

Let's contrast this with the approach of a competing organization that also offered quality services. Their clinical offerings were not as extensive as those of their competitor due to the fact that they chose to contribute time and resources in other areas. They built strong relationships with state agency leaders, they streamlined their admissions process, offered 24/7 referrals, and broadened their admission criteria.

Who ultimately won out? You guessed it, the organization that built strong relationships and offered fast and efficient admission service. On the surface this example is basic and obvious. However, if you look deeper you will see the presence of a model that speaks directly to the business needs of your referral sources. This is commonly referred to as the Business Motivation Model.

Business leaders want three main questions answered as they work toward achieving their mission and goals. They are:

1. **How do I increase revenue?**

    Increasing revenue can be accomplished in different ways depending on the needs of the organization. Companies can create significant market differentiation if they show how their services will improve the bottom line of their partners. Some examples of how to increase revenue are:
    - Increasing the number of successful admissions/clients
    - Improving payer mix or dollar value of a sale
    - Servicing larger audiences through an improved service model

2. **How do I reduce the cost of doing business?**

Business leaders are well aware that price is not always the answer when looking at decreasing costs, as there is a difference between cost and price. A negative effect of making decisions based on price alone would be choosing to go with the cheapest provider for creating a marketing campaign when the end result leads to the creation of an ineffective message and minimal reach with potential clients. This results in additional unexpected costs as a result of troubleshooting and a revision of your overall plan. Choosing a more expensive provider who offers more value and reliability would create savings and benefits that far outweigh the short-term difference in price.

3. **How do I improve the overall efficiency of my business?**

Businesses often improve their financial well-being by increasing overall efficiency. An organization may revamp its procurement process, improve the accuracy and efficiency of its billing methods, or streamline its services in an effort to build revenue. There are numerous ways a vendor can contribute to the bottom line by helping to improve overall efficiency of its business partners. This was exactly the approach taken by the residential program that chose to streamline its admissions process for the benefit of their referral sources.

Those who offer services that address the three business components just outlined are the organizations that ultimately win out. In this case, the latter organization understood that state agencies work on difficult cases and often struggle to find help in a timely manner. As a result, they broadened their admission criteria and developed a fast and efficient referral process. This change in service helped to increase the overall efficiency of the agencies that utilized residential services. In addition, employees of these agencies spent less time searching for appropriate placement for their clients. Thus, they were able to use this time to focus more on client needs, and this translated into higher quality services and improved measurable results for the agency.

In summary, this residential organization understood the business needs and profit model of its referral sources. It improved the overall efficiency of is partnering agencies, which in turn contributed to each agency's profit model, thus serving youth effectively! The result for the organization was a full census and a waiting list from several state agencies. It became the provider of choice and a trusted partner in the community by contributing to the bottom line of its partners.

Fear Not Numbers!

Using financial figures to explain your value proposition is the most effective way to engage and motivate business leaders. It is also one of the best ways to beat out your competition and win business.

A simple but powerful example would be a psychiatric organization looking to formalize a bed rate agreement with a large hospital. The organization generates buy-in from the prospective client by discussing cost savings for the prospect. And the best way to reach an agreement with a hospital CEO and CFO is to show them how your service will directly impact their bottom line. An example might look something like Table 7.1.

If you were selling these services and you were using a model similar to the one I just discussed, your summary might sound something like this: "This bed agreement contains no long lasting commitment on your part. You simply pay when you choose to use our services. The agreement creates a formal relationship between our two health care entities so that we can meet your needs

Table 7.1 *Cost/Benefit Analysis Example*

Cost/Benefit Analysis *Psychiatric Partnership Agreement*	
Estimates	**Cost/Savings**
10 psychiatric admissions per month serviced at your hospital at $1,000.00 per day *(average length of stay: 5 days per person)*	$55,000.00 monthly
Additional nursing staff: 30 hrs. per week at $18/hr	$2,160.00 monthly
Total cost per month	**$57,160.00 monthly**
Total cost per year	**$685,920.00 annually***
Use of our psychiatric inpatient services rate: $700 per day for 1 month	$35,000.00 monthly
Total cost per year if services used	**$420,000.00 annually**
Savings per month *(Differential between general hospital vs. psychiatric hospital)*	**$22,160.00 monthly**
Total savings per year	**$265,920.00 annually**

* This number does not include employee turnover; safety issues, injuries, impact on overall quality of care resulting from servicing psychiatric patients at the main hospital.

quickly and offer effective services to your patients. Based on the estimates you provided us this agreement will generate an immediate savings of $22,160 for the first month with a total savings of $265,920 in the first year. Keep in mind that this number is conservative in that it does not take into account the improvement in workplace productivity, quality of care, and the reduction in staff turnover."

The ultimate power of this approach is that there is no real selling involved. Once you show numbers in terms of revenue generated or cost savings businesses will have no choice but to buy!

CLIENT-BASED SELLING FOR ADMISSIONS DEPARTMENTS

Do you work in an organization whose success is highly dependent on front-end systems, processes, and people to feed the pipeline for your business? Wait, don't answer that because you and I already know the answer! Everyone is dependent on a customer service process that interacts effectively with potential clients. Without it there is no service or business to be conducted. I have seen businesses small and large fail due in large part to ineffective customer service on the front end of their service model. An excellent way to improve this important business function is to adopt the solution-focused and client-oriented sales model discussed at length in Chapter 3. The key elements of that model are:

- Sell the way clients want to buy
- Be present, listen, and ask questions
- Give value and offer solutions
- Be persuasive
- Go above and beyond

These principles offer organizations a powerful solution for marginal customer service by expanding the reach, scope, and power of your service model.

But don't take my word for it. Let's take a look at some common customer service positions, and you will begin to recognize opportunities where your organization can improve its customer service/sales model so you are building business opportunities rather than missing out on them.

"Sorry. It's Not in Our Scope."

This statement is a common response you will find in all industries, and it is a true killer in terms of business growth and development. It comes in many forms, such as, "We don't offer those services. Those are the responsibility of another organization so you need to contact them." Or how about this one, "The only option you have is this. If you don't do that, I cannot help you."

As a sales professional working for a private, for-profit behavioral health care organization I absolutely love when competitors take this approach with potential clients! Why? Because I know our organization can easily distinguish itself and make a lasting impression with prospects by simply being more customer-focused and adopting principles like giving value, offering solutions, and following through.

There is nothing essentially wrong with saying it is not a service you provide. It may in fact be completely removed from anything your organization offers. Take this example as a "for instance." What if you worked as a triage team member for a psychiatric hospital and someone called wanting tutoring services for their child? This is certainly out of scope for you, right? They are not requesting mental health services, and they don't need inpatient care. They want tutoring for a child having problems with mathematics and science. But what if we adopted some of the customer-focused sales principles and used them for this specific scenario? Is the question about tutoring services really out of scope then? If we take the viewpoint that "every situation is a selling opportunity," if we think long-term, if we look to give value and to sell the way customers want to buy, you will find that this parent's request is closer to a sales opportunity than you may have realized.

Don't believe me? Or do you think I'm being unrealistic? I understand that customer service positions in mental health are high stress and fast-paced jobs. However, your organization will ultimately choose to identify with this reality or decide to transcend and overcome the obstacles preventing it from being a best in class performer. I can guarantee that if your organization is not making this kind of effort to improve, another organization will; and when that happens, it will distance itself from you in the mind of the consumer.

Long-Term Benefits

Let's continue to challenge the thought that the initial call about tutoring was out of scope for a moment longer. Who was calling to inquire about tutoring services, and can you visualize what challenges and concerns they have? Perhaps it is a concerned parent who was referred to the psychiatric hospital by friends after doing a lot of talking in the community about his or her child's problems. Could it be possible that this child is in need of tutoring because of some behavioral and emotional problems? What if this child was a fine student until his father began drinking and his mother became depressed? Maybe environmental stressors led to the child becoming frightened, angry, and disillusioned. Would that not present an opportunity for mental health services?

I do not mean to imply that a customer service representative should always probe deeply in an effort to identify underlying needs, however, there are many instances where it is extremely effective and helpful to do just that. This is where the power of presence, listening, and asking good questions can make a difference between good customer service and outstanding customer service. But let's say that in-depth probing is not appropriate for this specific case. The mere act of being a valuable resource for the family will produce powerful long-term benefits for you and your organization.

Let me clarify further—if you choose to not immediately label the request as "out of scope," and you decide to offer value in some way, then you will have laid a foundation for a successful long-term relationship with that family. Therefore, instead of telling the parent you cannot help, you might politely say, "My organization does not offer tutoring, but let me ask you a few additional questions about your child, and I will see if I can find the best resource for you." After further discussion you tell the parent you are going to do some research and will get back with him or her shortly. You contact a few providers and then call back the parent with three referral options. You tell the parent you scheduled a tentative appointment for the child at one organization; because they had an unexpected cancellation, and initial appointments are typically booked months in advance due to lack of availability. This will certainly leave a different impression than the initial response, and once again you have sold your organization to this family!

Let's take this scenario even further. Since the family was highly impressed with your efforts, they talk with their friends and family about the organization. They might say, "You know, I called over there and they didn't offer those kinds of services, but they were so helpful and actually found some great resources to help my child." And what about the organizations you referred to the family? Let's say you found a large non-profit organization that offered tutoring for the community. Would they not be pleased that you thought of them? Do you think they might see a fair number of children who have mental health issues that contribute to struggles in school? Who do they currently refer to for treatment services and why? The fact that you are giving value to them will certainly make them consider your organization as a viable resource option. Let's also say that this organization has a large and powerful board of directors. What if they began hearing positive things about your organization as a result of your efforts?

The list of potential benefits goes on and on! And all because you chose not to say, "Sorry, we don't do that".

Exercise: Six Degrees to Behavioral Health
This is a great exercise you can have fun with as part of a customer service orientation program. It is very similar to the process we just went through with regard to the tutoring dilemma. I recommend using it to help develop a more

expansive customer service model and work culture. The content below helps to set some parameters for this exercise.

Exercise Purpose: To connect a scenario to a possible mental health need that your organization provides and to offer some form of help to the customer. You can do this in as many steps as possible. The need can be a hypothetical, and it can be future based. The only requirements being that the steps have a logical progression.

Points: A group of facilitators awards points for each team that successfully makes a positive connection and comes up with an effective solution/intervention:

Level 1 (1 point); Level 2 (2 points); Level 3 (3 points)

Steps:

1. Break up into two to four teams depending on the size of your group.
2. Give each team flip chart paper so they can write down their ideas.
3. Develop a series of index cards that present specific scenarios.
   Level 1: Contains more obvious scenarios that are easier to connect. (e.g., Do you offer a group on eating disorders?)
   Level 2: Contains more challenging topics. (e.g., Request for tutoring services)
   Level 3: Contains the most challenging and unrelated requests. (e.g., I am looking to sign up my child for T-ball)
4. A team member from one of the teams selects a card and reads it aloud.
5. The team has 10 minutes to discuss scenarios similar to the tutoring scenario presented above. They write down their steps and interventions on flip chart paper, and a group member presents their results.
6. The exercise facilitators choose to award points or not based on their efforts.
7. The team with the most points wins the challenge.

It's Not Us, It's Them

Years ago, I was a member of a collaborative venture involving a group of private non-profit organizations offering family services in a community-based format. Services included a parent education program, case management, and family counseling. Our team staffed cases on a weekly basis to discuss progress, and on one occasion we were complaining about a specific group of families who were part of the program but were not utilizing the services offered. One senior manager motioned to close the cases of all these families arguing that, "They don't want the services and show no motivation to change.

We can't help them if they don't want the services, so why bother following up with them? We need to close these cases and focus our attention on those who really want our help."

The reality of this scenario is that our collective frustration caused the entire team to personalize the inaction of these families. We felt our team had gone to great lengths to offer quality services to the community. As a result, when they were underutilized the families became our scapegoat. This approach is quite simply unacceptable in a world where business survival revolves around measurable results, cost savings, and revenue generation. Yes, we can make a case that some people refuse to access services even if they desperately need them. However, my response to that argument is—*so what?* Do we change the circumstances by resisting the reality of the situation? If we were not willing to accept the events as they currently existed, then I argue that our group was the one unwilling to change, not the families.

A smarter approach would involve looking at what one might be missing in terms of meeting customer needs. Are there barriers or obstacles preventing families from accessing services? If so, are they complex variables such as cultural issues preventing families from utilizing services or are they more practical issues such as lack of transportation or childcare? Are these the right services according to members of the community? If they are not, then what are the right services and why?

It goes back to the fundamental concept discussed earlier about the importance of creating a buying environment by removing barriers and creating want/need so people will buy. In this case, I believe our responsibility should have been to look at where the disconnect was in terms of what our team saw as valuable services and what families saw as nothing more than a hindrance.

Always remember the key principles involved in client-based selling. They will help you grow your business and improve your overall service quality.

- Sell the way clients want to buy
- Be present, listen, and ask questions
- Give value and offer solutions
- Arouse "need" in others
- Go above and beyond

SUMMARY

- Earn more business with organizations by understanding and speaking to the three key business questions important to all business leaders.

1. How do I increase revenue?
2. How do I reduce the cost of doing business?
3. How do I improve the overall efficiency of my business?

- When possible, create a powerful value proposition by using facts and figures that can clearly show savings offered and the possibilities for improving efficiency and increasing revenue. Create a "no choice but to buy" scenario for customers.
- Use client-based selling principles to improve on your organization's customer service skills.

PART THREE

The Future of Success

CHAPTER EIGHT

Social Networking in the Mental Health Profession

"The only thing we know about the future is that it will be different."

—Peter Drucker

Consider for a moment just how powerful you and I have become.

A *BusinessWeek* article in August 2005 chronicled the trials and tribulations of a man named Jeff Jarvis. Earlier that year, Mr. Jarvis was in need of a computer and ultimately chose a Dell for its reasonable price and Dell's solid reputation in the industry. There was one issue—his computer had problems, and a lot of them. He contacted Dell to fix his computer, but problems persisted.

It just so happened that Mr. Jarvis was one of thousands of people who actively embraced the ever-expanding social aspect of the Internet. But that's not the whole story. He was not only simply an active participant, he was a highly influential leader of a large online community. He cultivated and nurtured this community through his personal blog, buzzmachine.com. Mr. Jarvis used his passion and expertise for news and media to create a Web presence where people came to learn, to share, and to build relationships.

After months of frustration with his new computer, he decided to write a post on his personal blog about his experience. What happened next was astounding and important to note. The post hit a chord with people in communities across the country and beyond. Thousands of people replied to his post, and many others linked his post onto their blogs. People took notice, and as a result, so did more traditional news vehicles such as *BusinessWeek*. Soon his blog post was receiving so much traffic that a customer who googled Dell would see Jarvis's post and conversation right next to several Dell corporate links. Amazingly, the conversation was beginning to damage Dell's brand.

Jeff Jarvis' trials and tribulations offer us a window into the new economy.

I've already discussed, at length, the massive changes taking place across all markets where the power is shifting from the few to the many. However, this story speaks to a phenomenon of equal importance. And that phenomenon is the changing role and scope of social networks in the twenty-first century.

The Internet offers all of us a chance to be a part of something greater than ourselves. Like Jeff Jarvis, we have the ability to reach out, connect, and mobilize others. We can tell our stories or share our findings with people who can benefit from what we have to say. The Internet not only gives us a say, it allows us to build influence and credibility, and expand our reach as mental health professionals if we choose to take a chance.

As I mentioned in an earlier chapter, effective marketing is not about catchy phrases or slick advertisements. It's about being a part of a greater community and fostering life-long relationships. The Internet gives each and every one of us that opportunity. People are flocking to the Web in droves, and they're looking to be a part of something exciting, interesting, and new.

In mental health we are seeing the Internet play a more significant role at all levels, and it is beginning to serve as a critical entry point for people who are seeking help. When a family friend refers someone to a therapist in the community, that person is likely to search the Web to learn more about that therapist. If a mother of an autistic child is in need of resources, support, and guidance, she might find an online community that offers her all three. And the people in that community, whom the mother learns to trust, might suggest she contact a specific therapist who helped their children.

It is becoming more and more evident that a Web presence is important for success in our field. However, having a web site is not enough. Those who learn to embrace the social aspects of the Internet are the ones who will tap into the new marketplace and be rewarded for their efforts. They're the ones who will become most influential.

How Do I Find the Time?

How do practitioners get involved in social networking and still keep their focus on client work? Where's the work-life balance? These important questions are often ignored. It's easy to become overwhelmed and frustrated with social networking simply because there are so many options available. Where do you begin? An even better question would be, "Where do you end?"

Before giving up altogether on social networking and the World Wide Web, know that there are solutions. You may have opened a Facebook or Twitter account and see no value in these tools for your clinical practice. The fact is that these sites may or may not be the best option for you. Other social networking tools may be better suited for your goals. My goal, in the pages that follow, is to help clarify and demystify the social networking phenomenon for you.

The Internet can be an important part of your business if you understand what resources match up best with your needs and interests. Over the years I have learned what works best for my needs and this has given me the freedom to leave all the other technical "stuff" behind. I created a simple social networking model that enhanced my business goals while giving me the time and ability to focus on other initiatives. In addition, I learned to utilize web experts when necessary so that I had trusted partners to help make the Internet easier and more fun to use. You'll see exactly how I accomplished this as we move through this chapter, and you'll learn that you can create a similar strategy for yourself.

OVERVIEW

In this chapter I discuss the social networking aspects of the Internet and provide you with information and resources that will give you an opportunity to get involved. It's an exciting time to be in the field, and one of the reasons is the fact that the Internet offers a platform for whatever you are passionate about. The World Wide Web gives you the ability to powerfully market yourself and build a following by simply sharing your expertise.

But as I mentioned earlier, simply signing up for a Facebook account or getting people to follow you on Twitter does not mean you are using social networking in a way that can help you professionally. In fact, you may simply be wasting your time! Many marketing efforts and tools, both online and offline, fall on deaf ears not because they aren't useful but because they're not linked to a process that's focused on offering value and building trust. Social networking vehicles give you the opportunity to add value while at the same time enabling you to lead a community or movement. It can be a lot of fun and, most importantly, it can bring you untold levels of success if it is used effectively.

Let's take a look at some of these tools and see how best to use them within our profession.

BLOGGING FOR THE MENTAL HEALTH PROFESSIONAL

Years ago I asked myself a question that became the driving force for me professionally.

"What would happen if you integrated sophisticated sales and marketing principles into a mental health model?"

I wondered what kind of impact it might have on my ability to find interesting work and my ability to build a practice. It led to years of research and much of what you find in this book is the result of those efforts. My problem, however, was that my message reached only a small group of people based on my existing local networks. No matter how valuable my message, its reach was limited. That changed dramatically when I was introduced to the idea of blogging.

What is a blog, you ask. Good question. I had no idea a few years back. I heard people talk about blogs and blogging, but I never made much of an effort to understand what all the fuss was about.

The word blog is short for *web log*. At its most basic level, a blog is a web site that stores or logs online entries in reverse chronological order. In many ways it's similar to a journal where an individual or a group of individuals have the ability to post comments, write articles, or comment on any number of things they are interested in. Blogs also offer readers the ability to add their own comments and share their thoughts on whatever the blogger has chosen to write about that day. It is here that the social aspect of the tool truly comes into play.

A blog gives anyone the ability to share information with whomever is willing to listen. You might decide to set up a blog about your passion for gardening, your interest in renovating classic cars, or research you may be doing on a particular area of mental health. Viewers are then given an opportunity to participate and be a part of the conversation.

In earlier chapters I discussed traditional media being a risky investment in today's marketplace. My earlier argument was that resources have shifted from a scarcity model to one of seemingly infinite choice. In the past, when there had been a limited number of television stations and magazines, you could be assured of reaching a large percentage of the market through strategically placed advertisements. This is not the case today. There are simply too many choices, making it almost impossible to effectively reach your audience using a traditional marketing model. The solution now and in the future is to, in essence, build your own channel. Blogs provide you with the means to achieve this goal, and they can help grow your audience.

This mental health example clarifies things a bit further. Suppose you set up a blog based on the treatment of children with social anxiety. Your latest post focuses on the pros and cons of a relatively new medication that recently hit the market. You've treated several children who have been on this medication, and have gathered a fair amount of research on the efficacy of the medication. You decide to share your findings with the general public through a blog post. One outcome resulting from this post might be active participation from parents who read your post and appreciated your comments. Let's say there is a couple reading your blog, and their child was placed on this medication months ago. The medication worked wonderfully. They decide to share this experience with other readers by writing a follow-up comment to your original post. But perhaps another family was not so lucky, and they offer a follow-up comment about some of the side effects as a word of caution for parents. All of this would be important information families would find invaluable!

And as this conversation ensues you will notice that something very different is occurring from a marketing standpoint. You are no longer advertising your services in a traditional manner. You are now actively leading a community of people who are looking to share their stories. They are looking for support and guidance. You are providing the medium for them to participate and learn. In return, you learn from the participants, and you foster a community of people who value your input. A community of like-minded individuals grows and prospers. This is marketing in its highest form! It's what the writers of *The ClueTrain Manifesto* mean when they speak about new and more powerful forms of communication occurring that are based on open and honest feedback.

Best of all, when you choose to participate within a community at this level, you are not aggressively selling or marketing your services in the traditional sense. You are simply engaging in the social networking process, based on your genuine passion for a particular subject matter and your honest desire to help others.

After I explored the idea of blogging, I realized it would be a great way to share my message about the importance of sales and marketing for mental health professionals.

Throughout this chapter I use my experiences to introduce you to many of the social networking tools available. I recommend that you also take a look at my blog at www.davidpdiana.com. It will give you a better idea of what I am talking about and how I chose to use all the latest Internet tools in my marketing efforts.

Blogging Resources

One of the great things about choosing to have a blog is that you can set one up free of charge. All you'll need to pay for is hosting. Many companies offer templates you can use quickly and easily. In addition, they give you the ability to edit your own content without the need of a web developer. You don't need to know how to write code to post an article or to add a link or image. It's all right there for you! I chose to use a WordPress template, but there are several great companies offering blogging services, and my guess is that these resources will continue to expand in the years to come.

Here are just a few blog resources I'd recommend you look into:

- Wordpress.com
- Tumblr.com

- Typepad.com
- Blogspot.com

It's important to note that, even though there are plenty of free resources available, there are a lot of advantages to hiring a good web developer and/ or graphic designer. I began by using a free WordPress template, but when I wanted to get more sophisticated I turned to a web designer. A good web designer can customize your blog or web site in a way that will make it stand out. He or she can also help you make sense of the growing number of tools and services available today. My developer suggested I look at an upgraded WordPress template so I would have added functionality and a better design. I paid a small one-time fee for a new template and had my designer add graphics and do some general customization. The result, shown in Figure 8.1, is what you see today at www.davidpdiana.com.

Figure 8.1 My WordPress Blog

Once I launched my site, I e-mailed friends and colleagues telling them about its existence. I then made a commitment to write a blog post once a week about sales and marketing skills and resources for mental health professionals. And with that, I wrote my first post, shown in Table 8.1.

That was it. I was on my way. I had no mechanisms for attracting traffic to my site, and as a result, no more than five to ten people read my initial post. But I took the first step, I took a chance on something I was excited about, and it has made all the difference in the long run.

Blogging is by no means the only social networking tool, and it is not for everyone. But it remains my favorite Internet tool. I enjoy it for a number of

Table 8.1 My First Blog Post

Entering the Blogosphere!

Welcome to my first official blog post. I have now entered into the unchartered waters of 100+ million bloggers worldwide. This is an alarming statistic when you consider the fact that only five years earlier the number was listed at five million. Talk about missing the boat!

And yet, my effort to blog as a mental health professional and to blog on this particular topic is, in fact, a rather unique effort. Why? Well, precisely for the same reasons that I have become so invested in researching sales and marketing concepts for mental health professionals - because while 100 million people have a blog in some way, shape or form very few in our industry are actually a part of that astounding figure.

This blog is designed to offer readers in the mental health field useful tips, resources and insights pertaining to sales, marketing and business development ideas. My hope is that it will contain information that will be of direct benefit to your career in the field. So…

> - If you find yourself trapped in a state mental health system on the verge of sweeping change then this blog is for you.
> - If you're a successful private practitioner looking to expand or make your business life easier then the information here will be of considerable interest.
> - And if you are looking for work without success and asking yourself why in the world you ever chose to enter this field I say fear not! This blog will offer information that will help you find opportunities you may never have known existed.

I look forward to sharing all that I uncover! Look for my next post in one week.

David

---

reasons, but perhaps the greatest benefit I get from this activity has nothing to do with the number of subscribers or the number of people who visit my blog. Blogging, for me, has created a shift in how I approach my profession. It has given me a vehicle to express myself creatively and has given me a level of discipline I did not have in the past.

The benefits of blogging are many.

- It gives you a highly effective marketing tool.
- It expands your network well beyond your local area.
- It provides a platform for you to promote and sell your services and products.
- It introduces you to new business opportunities and new people with like-minded interests.
- It builds credibility that makes you more influential in the marketplace.
- It helps crystallize your vision, message, and career path.
- It sharpens your skills and builds expertise.

In short, if you have something to say, blogging gives you the ability to do so. It doesn't matter if you're selling coffee, real estate, or mental health services. The opportunity to have a voice and build a following is available to you right now and it's a lot easier to set up than you may think.

I Have a Blog. Now What?

If you've decided to start a blog, congratulations! You're in for a fun ride. But it will take some time and dedication if your blog is to become a successful marketing tool. In the beginning, I wrote posts that reached very few people, and it stayed that way for several months. But there are things you can do to add impact quickly. Here are just a few basic tips I believe are important if you're trying to build a presence online through your blog or web site.

Give away more information than you think you should.

You may think you're already giving people enough value. Perhaps you offer a resource list or links to interesting articles. But I'm talking about offering value that will surprise people. One way to accomplish this is to create a written work that maps out what you believe in and what you are passionate about. Then, give it away free to your viewers. Blog experts refer to this material as "flagship content." This content should be compelling enough to entice people to visit your site because of this free offering, and then tell their colleagues to come take a look as well.

Focus on what you believe in, not on the financial possibilities.

A lot of people work on building an online presence to cash in or create a passive income stream. I hear this over and over again from people who are looking at the Internet as an opportunity. They have an idea for a product, and they want to package and sell it online, they want to set up a paid members only area, or they want to charge for the content they have created. In my experience, these ideas are great but only if they are a part of something bigger. You have to be in it for the right reasons and build a foundation of trust and credibility before you can offer something people will buy online or offline. If you don't do this, people will view what you are offering as a smoke screen, and they'll be right! Remember the sales lessons from the earlier chapters of this book — the best selling involves a long-term relationship building process.

Make it as easy as possible for people to follow and communicate with you.

Blogs and other social networking tools offer you yet another way to build your network. Take steps to ensure your blog gives people a chance to talk openly and honestly with you. And give them choices about how they might like to do so.

You've got to reach out!

This tip is obvious enough that we tend to take it for granted. I see it all the time. People decide to see what social media is all about, they set up accounts with various social networking tools, and then they give up soon after because they don't see results. If you are not willing to engage in conversations and reach out to others, what makes you think others will reach out to you? Social networking is a two-way process. It requires you to listen in on conversations and to actively participate. Find out what people are doing online and engage them in conversations. Learn from what they are doing and help support them. You must get yourself out there if anyone is going to notice.

As time went by, I began searching for other ways to reach out to my target market online. I looked into Facebook, Twitter, LinkedIn, and many others. After months of research I chose to add a Twitter account and an e-mail subscription service to my blog, thereby expanding my reach and making it easier for people to follow what I was doing.

One of the main reasons I like having a blog is that it serves as a central hub for other social networking tools. I favor an approach where you choose two or three social networking tools you like and link them to one another so they all work together. If you visit my blog, you have several choices. You can follow me on Twitter and receive updates whenever something new is posted to my site, or you can choose to sign up and receive e-mail updates. Together these choices create a networked system of communication that reaches out to a large audience of interested readers.

No matter what social networking tool you use, there is always the challenge of engaging readers and drawing them to your site.

In the beginning, it will involve a real grassroots effort where you inform your network and begin promoting the site at events, trainings, and the like. Some people like to talk about the importance of Search Engine Optimization (SEO) but I prefer a different approach. Yes, SEO is important, but climbing to the top of the Google charts can be a costly proposition. I believe in the idea of offering a high quality product and/or service, reaching out to other communities, and staying committed to that process. When you do this, you will eventually find your audience.

So now you have a blog or a web site and you're working on promoting it. Let's take a closer look at some web applications that will help get you where you'd like to go.

UNDERSTANDING RSS FEEDS

Like most people, I have a wide variety of personal and professional responsibilities. So how do I prioritize my time, and how do people earn my attention? It's hard to be heard when everyone is so inundated with information and responsibilities.

I faced this problem when looking for information online. I didn't have time to search for interesting and unique content on the Internet. If, for instance, I went to your web site and found it very informative and helpful, I still might never visit it again. Why? There are too many reasons to name here, but I can tell you that one of the reasons would *not* be because I didn't want to visit. I would love to return to your site, but perhaps I forgot you existed, or I kept putting it off because it felt like too much of a time waster to see if you were offering anything new.

Enter RSS Feeds

An RSS feed stands for "Really Simple Syndication." It gives a web reader the ability to say, "I like the information given on this site and I'd like to be reminded whenever the site is updated." Many news-related sites, blogs, and other online publishers syndicate their content as an RSS feed to whoever wants it.

RSS feeds can be read using software called an RSS reader. The RSS reader checks the user's subscribed feeds regularly for new work and downloads any updates that it finds. Web sites, blogs and web browsers then provide a user interface to monitor and read these feeds.

A person can access this feature by clicking on an icon similar to the one you see in Figure 8.2. This RSS icon indicates that a web feed is present on a specific

Figure 8.2   The RSS Icon

web page, and a person can receive updated information from that page if they choose to get the feed.

Still unclear about RSS Feeds? Here's a great response I received from my web developer at samedis.com when I asked him to define RSS feeds. It should be noted that while his analogy really helped me understand how feeds operate, there is a whole lot more to the process than meets the eye. This example, however, is perfect for our purposes, as there's no need to get bogged down in all the technical details.

Perhaps a good way to think of an RSS Feed is like the AP wire (Associated Press). The AP wire contains just the raw content that's published by the AP. Newspapers and magazines that pay for it can then take that content and package it up nicely into a newspaper column or a magazine page. When you use WordPress, or any blogging tool, to write content you're outputting an RSS feed which contains the raw content (like the AP Wire). Your blog software (e.g., WordPress, Typepad, Blogspot) packages that up with its templates and styles it into a nice looking blog.

So what value does this offer? For starters, people use feeds to filter and obtain content on the Web that they want without the need to constantly search for it. It's a very efficient way to obtain news and information online.

More importantly, an RSS feed adds a new level of interactivity that keeps you in front of your target audience. Rather than waiting and hoping for people to visit your site, you actively engage your viewers. It is this functionality that has allowed me to remain actively involved with several blogs and web sites on the Internet. Without this functionality, these sites might very well have lost me as a reader long ago.

RSS feeds are powerful marketing tools that will enhance your efforts to grow your business and mental health career by building a community of users who hear your message time and time again.

Online Newsletter Subscription Tools

As time went by I learned about more powerful ways to use an RSS feed, and this is where newsletter subscriptions and e-mail came into play.

In my opinion, the best tools available to you online are those that offer a subscription-based service for your customers. I've already stressed the fact that it's difficult to get people to actively come to your site of their own free will. We know people are busy juggling all sorts of responsibilities, and they are constantly inundated with information. Subscription-based services help address this challenge and work to build a community of committed web readers. These services accomplish this by reaching out to people through one of the most powerful communication tools used today—e-mail.

Once I built the framework for my blog I chose to write an online newsletter and offered readers the ability to sign up to receive the newsletter free of charge. If someone came to my site, read some of my posts, and liked what I had to say, there would be a high probability they would provide their e-mail address in order to receive the newsletter. The result—my user list expanded along with my market reach and influence.

The process I used represents one of the keys to good web design. Good web sites or blogs have pages with purpose. Each web page is designed to engage viewers in a certain way with the hope that they will take some sort of action. The web visitor might take action by bookmarking the page or by telling a friend. And if you use other forms of web technology, that same visitor might take the first big step to becoming a valuable member of your community by choosing to become a registered member of the site.

Think about the implications of this model for our profession and for you specifically!

Let's say you're a private practitioner specializing in the treatment of eating disorders. You promote your practice through community trainings and through various other marketing channels. All the while, you make a concerted effort to ensure your marketing efforts draw people to your web site. Why? Because you want to engage interested people for the long term.

Your target audience might be impressed with a newspaper interview you gave or a seminar you led, but then what happens? They make a mental note of your services and move on with their lives. You're off their radar screen. However, what if you set up a web site or blog that offers updated information about adolescent development, peer pressure, self-esteem, and body image? Or let's say you also include tips and resources on healthy eating habits. You might even choose to interview people who are doing interesting research on eating disorders or who have important stories to tell based on their experiences. You engage people in real and important discussions about a topic you are an expert in. And after offering all this, you give them the option of signing up to receive updates focusing on all the areas I have just listed. It's a very enticing and value-driven proposition. Best of all, it addresses the "out of sight, out of mind" dilemma. You reach out to a community of registered users who expect and want information from you. This is the kind of long-term and lasting effect an online subscription based model offers you.

And best of all, you will have fostered a deep and significant relationship with the people in your community. If you have done all this successfully, whom do you think they'll contact when someone they know has problems with self-esteem or body image?

Hopefully, I've convinced you to take a look at some of these services. Here are some interesting subscription based tools I believe deserve a closer look.

Feedburner.com

Feedburner is an RSS feed tool with an e-mail feature. Its core function is to give your web site e-mail subscription capabilities. Feedburner allows users to sign up and receive e-mail updates every time you post new information. Instead of having updates sent to a person's browser (like a traditional RSS feed) it goes to their e-mail. It also gives you "traffic analysis" capabilities, meaning you can generate reports to see how many people visited your site and what pages they viewed.

However, Feedburner is not a dedicated newsletter tool, and therefore, it makes things difficult when you're looking for more advanced subscriber management capabilities. Feedburner doesn't have any tools to import, segment, or otherwise manage subscribers, nor does it have any detailed reporting about who received, opened, or clicked through the e-mail.

Feedburner is a great service, but if you're looking for something more robust, tools like MailChimp and Mad Mimi are excellent alternatives.

Both of these are e-mail newsletter tools with an RSS feature. According to my web developer,

> Online newsletter tools like MailChimp and MadMimi do exactly the same thing as a Blog, they take your RSS feed and package it up into a nice looking e-mail. They then leverage their newsletter engine to send that email out to all of your subscribers.

MadMimi.com

Mad Mimi is a great e-mail marketing company that gives you the ability to create branded, well-designed newsletters and promotions. I use Mad Mimi for my e-mail marketing campaigns and I highly recommend them. If you have a blog and are looking to build a following, then Mad Mimi can help you achieve your goals.

How, you say? If I'm looking to build an online presence I might create an e-book and choose to offer it free to people who subscribe to my blog. Mad Mimi gives you the ability to create opt-in boxes so people can sign up to receive the offer. Better yet, you also have the ability to create auto-responders. What does this mean? Let's say someone becomes a registered member of your blog and receives your free e-book. Through Mad Mimi, you can create automated follow-up e-mail campaigns that serve as powerful sales and marketing tools. Once someone registers on your site, you can create a follow-up e-mail that is sent one week from the time a person becomes a registered member. The e-mail thanks the person for registering and invites them to sign up for an online seminar or in-person workshop you are giving. This is just one simple example of the power of e-mail marketing.

Mad Mimi is easy to use, cost-effective, and also happens to offer the best customer service and support in the marketplace. You will be amazed at the attention and support you receive. I continue to be amazed! Give them a call, tell them I sent you, and see how they might help make your online dreams a reality.

MailChimp.com

MailChimp is another e-mail marketing company that offers a very robust newsletter tool with an RSS feed feature. It is pricier than Mad Mimi, but MailChimp does a great job and offers an excellent product.

❧

There are several other newsletter tools you can choose from, such as iContact and Constant Contact. You can explore those on your own; and if you choose to use one of these tools you are well on your way to improving your marketing efforts while having fun at the same time!

What makes these tools so powerful is the fact that they take the feed concept a step further. Rather than searching for content and information that is filtered through a person's web browser (like a traditional RSS feed), you send your content directly to people's e-mail accounts. And for busy adults who are inundated with information, e-mail messages are very effective ways to ensure you are being seen and heard.

Figure 8.3 provides a quick look at what my blog's subscription-based model looks like. When visitors come to my site they can enter their information in

Figure 8.3 My E-Mail Subscription Marketing Model

the sign-up section. My blog posts and free e-books add value and engage visitors so that they choose to be part of this unique online community.

TWITTER AND THE MENTAL HEALTH PROFESSION

Everyone seems to be talking about Twitter, and while no one knows where this emerging technology is headed, we do know that it has become an international phenomenon. Originally, I had no idea what Twitter could possibly do for my mental health career. All I knew was that it was becoming more and more popular as a social networking tool, and therefore, I decided to open an account to see what all the fuss was about.

And then what? Well—I had no idea!

"Do I tell people I'm going to dinner? Should I inform them about an interesting show I saw on TV last night? Why would anyone care?"

I still had not quite grasped what Twitter was all about.

Twitter is a free social networking service that allows people the ability to stay connected and to communicate in real time. Twitter's own web site defines itself this way:

Twitter is a service for friends, family, and co-workers to communicate and stay connected through the exchange of quick, frequent answers to one simple question: What are you doing?

It accomplishes this by giving you the ability to create your own profile, free of charge, whereby you can send and read tweets, which are text-based posts limited to 140 characters in length. These tweets are delivered to and viewed by those people who have chosen to follow you on Twitter.

Slowly but surely, I started to see how I could make Twitter work for me.

One of the first things I learned was that I could add Twitter to my blog as a networking and communication tool (Blog companies like WordPress have easy-to-use features to help you do this). If someone clicked on the Twitter icon on my site to follow me, then every time I posted new content on my blog, this person would receive a tweet from me with a link to my post.

Figure 8.4 shows you a portion of my blog that contains all three of the social networking tools I use today: (1) Follow me on Twitter; (2) Receive my RSS feed; and/or (3) Subscribe to get e-mail updates.

Twitter provided my visitors with another option to stay connected, and it has had a profound impact on my blog's visibility. Once I made Twitter a functional

SUBSCRIBE

RSS Feed

Get Updates via Email

Figure 8.4   Three Ways to Stay Connected on My Blog

part of my site I began to get new followers daily. I was starting to get increasing traffic on my blog, and the number of people giving me permission to speak with them online was growing exponentially. My blog posts were now reaching an ever-expanding audience.

This is where Twitter can add value for you. Twitter and other social networking tools can strengthen your efforts to expand your network and your presence. When you reach a critical point in terms of followers who believe in what you have to say and are committed to your cause, you have the flexibility to offer a wide array of services and market them to people who truly want and need your expertise.

Still unsure about Twitter? Here are a few ways I think mental health professionals can leverage Twitter. If you use Twitter correctly, you could be amazed by the results.

- Use Twitter as a market research tool: Ask people what they want from a therapist and what they feel is missing in the marketplace.
- Go to search.twitter.com and type in a mental health topic of interest to you. Twitter gives you a list of discussions currently taking place on the topic you chose. Start participating in these discussions!
- Tweet about your area of expertise.
- Offer quality resources focusing on your area of expertise.
- Use Twitter as a press release tool for key functions you and others are delivering.
- Re-tweet good content others have offered and spread their message.
- Introduce yourself and ask if there is anything you can do for others.
- Offer straight talk about the field (e.g., medications, therapy, disorders, signs, and symptoms)

My discussion of Twitter is not intended as a comprehensive technical review, rather its purpose is to show you how a social networking tool like Twitter can benefit you in your business development efforts.

Figures 8.5 through 8.11 contain some useful Twitter tips to help get you started.

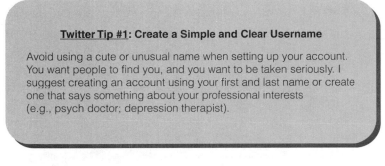

Twitter Tip #1: Create a Simple and Clear Username

Avoid using a cute or unusual name when setting up your account. You want people to find you, and you want to be taken seriously. I suggest creating an account using your first and last name or create one that says something about your professional interests (e.g., psych doctor; depression therapist).

Figure 8.5 Twitter Tip #1

Twitter Tip #2: Use a Professional Picture

I see a lot of Twitter profiles where people choose to use graphics or "strange" pictures of themselves. This makes it hard to build a connection or any level of trust online. Even homemade digital headshots are something you might want to reconsider. A professionally done headshot is a nice distinguishing feature. Take a look at other mental health professionals on Twitter. How many of them have a professional photograph as part of their profile? Trust me, you'll make a lasting impression with one.

Figure 8.6 Twitter Tip #2

Twitter Tip #3: Focus on Value for Others vs. Self Promotion

It's tempting to send all kinds of tweet messages that talk about what you are doing and what you would like to promote. However, I encourage you to think long-term in your approach. Use Twitter to foster a community by offering resources and information that people find helpful and fascinating. Get people to talk about you before you start talking about yourself.

Figure 8.7 Twitter Tip #3

Twitter Tip #4: Send Messages to Specific People

When you set up a Twitter account, there is an open text field at the top of the web page where you can type in your Tweets. You send a message to your followers by hitting the "Update" button.

But what if you'd like to send a Tweet to a specific person? All you need to do is use the "@" sign along with that person's username when you begin your Tweet. If, for example, you'd like to send me a personal message, you would start your post: "@davidpdiana/ was wondering if you have additional information on the research you reference on your site?" There is also a link on your profile page in the right hand column where you can view all your personal messages. My link would read: @davidpdiana.

Figure 8.8   Twitter Tip #4

Twitter Tip #5: Find Your Audience Using Twitter Directories and Search Tools

Mrtweet.com and **Twellow.com** are my favorites. Both are great tools for finding people you are interested in meeting on Twitter.

Mr. Tweet is a free Twitter service where you can choose your target audience and learn who is out there. You simply enter in specific keywords and Mr. Tweet provides you with profiles of people who you might be interested in following. I have connected with some facinating people using this service, and it has led to new customers and business partners.

Twellow.com positions itself as the Twitter yellow pages. It's a great directory where you can search for people in your target market. It offers an opportunity to search quickly and easily.

Figure 8.9   Twitter Tip #5

Twitter Tip #6: Promote Other People

A woman once sent me a Tweet with some great advice and valuable resources she thought I might enjoy. So what did I do? I took the time to let my followers know how helpful she was, and I made an effort to promote her work and her website. She in turn promoted my resources and blog to her followers.

Figure 8.10   Twitter Tip #6

> **Twitter Tip #7**: Make the Effort to Follow People on Twitter
>
> As I mentioned earlier in this chapter, you have to engage others before they engage you. Don't make the assumption that people will simply follow you. In addition, don't get hung up on whether you are following more people than are following you. In order to get the word out, you have to make the first move and reach out to others. You'll be surprised whom you meet and what opportunities come your way.

Figure 8.11   Twitter Tip #7

Twitter is a fascinating tool; take some time to try it out for yourself. I believe it has significant value for mental health professionals looking to increase their visibility. In addition, it gives us a glimpse into the future, where people use new tools and technology to reach out and connect with others on a scale that was unimaginable ten years earlier.

I'm looking forward to seeing who the trailblazers are going to be in our field. Who are the ones who will learn how to use a tool like Twitter to effectively grow their mental health business?

BUSINESS NETWORKING AND ONLINE FORUMS

It should be quite obvious at this point that today's Internet has evolved into a dynamic social medium where people come together to share ideas, meet one another, build relationships, and offer support. Blogging, the use of subscription-based models, and tools like Twitter all have the ability to add richness to the work you do.

Surprisingly, the world of social media does not end there. Here are some other excellent and interesting options to consider.

LinkedIn.com

LinkedIn is a social networking site for business professionals, and it is used primarily for professional networking purposes. I know many business professionals who use LinkedIn to build their networks and to stay connected. It is also an effective promotional tool where you can uncover new business opportunities by engaging in conversations with like-minded professionals.

The professional networking capabilities alone make LinkedIn worth your while, but I believe there is more to the story. LinkedIn, and other social media platforms, speak to a fundamental shift in the job search market. Everyone has the ability to promote their services and build their personal brand via the Internet, and I believe that it is now no longer a choice but a necessity. If you are looking to grow your career or are unemployed and actively looking for work, then LinkedIn is an important place to be. Resumes are old news. More and more employers are turning to LinkedIn to see who you are. Do you have a blog? If so, what are you saying about your field of expertise? Have clients and colleagues offered recommendations (an important feature on LinkedIn)? When you answer these questions positively, you become much more attractive to employers.

LinkedIn also offers users the ability to create or participate in online forums. It is easy, and it's free. Once you register on the site you have the ability to search existing groups or to create your own. As an example, I know a psychiatrist who has a LinkedIn group focusing on resources, wellness skills, and treatment options for people suffering from mood disorders. Within this group mental health professionals offer guidance and support to community members who are suffering from depression or Bipolar Disorder. All kinds of great information is shared and everyone gains from the experience.

Facebook.com

Facebook is yet another widely used tool that many businesses are beginning to explore as a way to communicate with customers. Organizations use Facebook to keep people informed about business initiatives and to get honest feedback from consumers.

Earlier in this chapter I picked on Dell, but let's also give them some credit. They learned the hard way about the power of social networks. Since that incident a few years ago, they have made significant efforts to communicate with consumers via social media. If you did a search on Facebook for Dell, you'd find several Dell Facebook pages, one of them dedicated solely to consumer issues. Now, if you have a problem with your Dell computer, you can vent on their Facebook page. And you know what will happen? In addition to other consumers offering tips on how to troubleshoot the situation, you will also be contacted by a Dell employee who will work very hard to address your problem.

There are all kinds of Facebook pages you can create but the key to success is offering a vehicle that helps communities come together. If you'd like to see how the world of psychology and Facebook come together, I suggest you do a keyword search to see what communities are out there. You'll find some interesting Facebook sites for eating disorders, mood disorders, and all sorts of mental health topics. And when you search these sites, ask yourself what these communities are doing well or not so well. Is there an opportunity for you to create your own community?

Facebook also offers a **Fan Page** feature and this appears to be where the real gold is for businesses and professionals. If you're looking to reach out to potential clients or business partners, then a Facebook Fan Page should be part of your marketing strategy and plan. You can create any number of fan pages depending on your needs. For example, if you are holding a two-day workshop in the coming months, you can create a fan page and use it as a promotional tool. If you are opening a new practice, you can create a page and use it as part of a promotional campaign.

Once someone becomes a fan, it links up to their Facebook News Feed so that all their friends will be able to read your content. This feature ensures your information is reaching an ever-expanding network. In addition, Fan Pages give you the ability to send announcements to your fans at any time, making it a great e-mail marketing tool.

Ning.com (A Social Networking Platform)

Ning is another interesting social networking tool. It's a great application in that it gives you the ability to create a your own social networking site in a matter of minutes. As an example, if you're an expert in Grief Therapy, you can create a social networking site on that very topic using Ning. Once you set up an account through Ning, you are given a site template with a variety of social networking features. For example, web visitors who come to your site will be able to register for free, create their own profiles with pictures, create community discussions, contribute articles, and add members to their friend list. In addition, a Ning template gives users the ability to share resources, offer book suggestions, and even submit their own blog posts.

Of course, you don't have to create your own social networking site to take advantage of Ning as a business opportunity. You can simply participate in one that already exists and, again, get your name out there.

Two Ning sites for mental health professionals worth exploring are Links for Shrinks (http://linksforshrinks.ning.com) and the Online Therapy Institute (http://onlinetherapyinstitute.ning.com). Take a look at these two sites, and you will see all the functionality available to you.

What I find so fascinating about social networking and technology in general is that it allows you to reach out to people in ways, and at a scale, that was not possible in years prior.

And now that you have some information about the kinds of tools available I suggest you explore these resources for yourself. Pay attention to new trends, and see what tools you like and dislike. The Internet and social networking is evolving at an incredibly fast pace. Six months from now there will no doubt be new opportunities and resources. Give some of these new tools a try and see how they might play a role in the work you do. You can define an online strategy that suits your comfort level and you can do so without compromising your time or your commitment to the therapeutic process.

Take advantage of this window of opportunity. Spread your message, find people who believe in what you have to say, and lead an online community. It will enrich you both personally and professionally.

SUMMARY

- The Internet offers all of us a chance to be a part of something greater than ourselves. The Internet not only gives us a say, it allows us to build influence and credibility, and expand our reach as mental health professionals at a level never seen before.
- Blogging is one of the most powerful social networking tools available and it is a great fit for mental health professionals. There are a wide array of resources you can use to set up your blog free of charge.
- Some helpful tips when blogging are:
  1. Give away valuable information to help you build a following (e.g., free e-book, resource list).
  2. Focus on your beliefs and passion for a particular topic. Don't focus on the financial possibilities.
  3. Leverage tools that make it easy for people to follow you and hear your message.
  4. Actively reach out to others and engage in online discussions.
- Newsletter subscriptions on your web site or blog are excellent tools for marketing your services. They allow you to use a permission-based marketing model.
- MadMimi and MailChimp are two excellent newsletter subscription services worth considering.
- Tools like Twitter and Facebook are only effective networking tools when they are a part of a greater overall marketing plan.
- Ning.com is an organization that gives you the ability to create a free online community. It is easy, free, and a great way to market yourself online.

CHAPTER NINE

Selling Yourself in Today's Job Market

It had been six months of frustration and disappointment. Six months searching for a new job with few options and limited results. Until one day, my friend (we'll call him Jason) received a call about an opportunity that seemed both interesting and promising. He had an initial screening interview conducted by the department manager, and it went well. The second round interview was conducted in panel format. The competition for this position seemed tough, but he prepared well and could feel his excitement build at the prospect of landing this job. Jason left the panel interview quite optimistic. He answered all their questions well, and the CEO seemed impressed. The CEO's excitement leaked out on a few occasions as she began to talk about growth of the program as if Jason were already a part of the team. Jason just had a feeling he had done well and would get an offer. Two days later he received a call from the assistant executive director offering him the job!

"Jason, we were all impressed with your experience and your treatment philosophy, and as a result, we would like to offer you the position as Clinical Director. As we mentioned earlier, you will be responsible for the management of two treatment programs and will be supervising a staff of seven employees."

He enthusiastically replied, "Thank you! I enjoyed meeting the entire leadership team and am really excited about being a part of the organization."

The assistant executive director continued, "Great. The offer for this position is $37,000 annually with benefits."

Jason had secretly dreaded this moment. Everything seemed a great fit, but he knew, based on past experience, that there was still one big hurdle—and that was salary. And there it was. His worst fears were validated as she told him the offer. He took a deep breath and stumbled over his next statement, "I am excited about the opportunity but was looking for something a bit higher in terms of salary."

She responded by saying, "Unfortunately, we don't have any room to negotiate. A portion of the monies allotted for this position are grant funded, which restricts our ability to negotiate."

"Is there room for salary growth based on performance?" he asked.

She paused, "Not really. Our organization has looked into this. We may be able to offer a small increase to about $39,000 in years 3 and 4 of the grant, but that is all. This is one of our highest paid positions."

"What about a cost of living increase?" he asked

"Other than what I just told you, there are no more funds for the position. In addition, since we want to ensure these programs are a success, we are requiring a two-year commitment by the person who accepts the position."

At the time of this real-life scenario, Jason was an eight-year veteran in the industry with management skills, a track record for success, and excellent references. This was the third opportunity he applied to where he was offered a salary that was virtually impossible for him to take. And yet, Jason remembers contemplating the offer for a few days following his conversation with the assistant executive director. After all, who knows what else is out there? He thought that perhaps if he took the position and paid his dues, other opportunities in the organization would arise after two years. He began to question his worth and value. And then Jason began to rationalize.

"Well, we're in this field to help others, not to make a lot of money."

Thankfully, he chose not to take the position and instead continued his search. It was a long process, but one that was worthwhile, as it gave him the chance to hone his job search skills, learn better ways to promote himself, and uncover better opportunities in the mental health industry.

I mention this example because even now, I hear from people in the profession who rationalize in the same manner Jason had years ago. And my message to you in this chapter is: Do not do this!

You do not have to settle or rationalize your way into a position or career path where you compromise your value. There are opportunities in mental health where you can achieve your goals, but to do so you must take a different approach and conduct your search in a different manner. It's easier than you might think, and here's a more uplifting example to show you how it can be accomplished using many of the sales and marketing principles I have already discussed.

WHAT THE FUTURE OF JOB SEARCHING LOOKS LIKE

In a previous chapter I briefly mentioned the professional challenges I was faced with while living in Boston and trying to make a living as a mental health practitioner. It was at this time that a friend and former classmate in graduate school was beginning his own job search and it produced some phenomenal results. I'd like to share his story with you because it's a story about what an effective job search should look like both now and in the future.

His story begins in similar fashion as mine. There were very few career opportunities at a level he felt he needed to grow and support a family. He lived in Washington, DC and had a very good job that paid quite well by mental health standards. He was, in fact, a director for a large program. He managed well over 40 employees and worked long hours. After four years in that role, he was beginning to become emotionally and psychologically exhausted. He wanted out. Each day he found himself becoming more and more depressed. Over the course of several months, we shared our job search war stories. Like me, he couldn't find any good opportunities.

One day, he got lucky and met a CEO for a large private behavioral health care company in the area. They hit it off, and the CEO invited him in for an interview. He loved the people and did well during the interview process. The problem he wrestled with, however, was the fact that the position they were offering was identical to what he was already doing. After a few days of soul searching he decided the risk was far greater than the reward. "Why jump from the frying pan and into the fire?" he thought. At least he knew what to expect with his current job. The result—he regretfully declined the offer and continued his search.

At that time, he and I spoke daily, mostly to vent. He, like myself, continued to find no opportunities. Another month passed, and he became desperate, telling me he was going to cold call some of the managers and executives he had spoken with months prior. One of those people was the CEO he had recently turned down. He left a voicemail saying, "I know things didn't work out with the previous opportunity, but I still believe I'd be a great fit in your organization and want to see if we can talk about other opportunities that might be available."

An hour later he had a return call from the CEO inviting him to dinner. "We were just talking about you and were excited when you called back," he said. "I'd like to invite you to dinner with some of our leadership team so we can talk about the possibility of you joining us."

My friend was overjoyed. He met the CEO, COO, and medical director at a fancy downtown restaurant. They ordered wine, appetizers, and expensive entrees. Then the CEO paused for a moment and said, "The job is still yours if you want it."

My friend was confused. "I'm sorry. I don't understand," he said.

"We still have not been able to fill the Director position so we were excited to hear you were still interested. The job is yours if you want it."

My friend's heart sank and his stomach churned. "I'm sorry, but I must have misunderstood. I thought we were meeting to talk about new opportunities with your organization, not the one I interviewed for previously."

Unfortunately, the CEO informed him, they didn't have other opportunities. So there sat my friend, at the beginning of a meal, sipping wine and eating an expensive dinner paid for by a potential employer, knowing that he could not and would not take the same job he had already turned down. After an hour of discussions he finished the longest dinner of his life. He got up and the CEO approached him.

The CEO said, "We're disappointed this is not for you, but we're having a hell of a time finding someone for this position. If you know of anyone good please let us know."

And at that, he was off. My friend called me the following day to tell me how down and out he felt on his ride home that night. There were limited opportunities available to him and he felt he just committed career suicide by turning down the largest behavioral health care employer in the area—twice in two months!

But then he thought about what the CEO said to him:

"We're disappointed this is not for you but we're having a hell of a time finding someone for this position. If you know of anyone good, please let us know."

What if he actually followed through on this? No one usually would. It was something people said, a social formality. He felt he had nothing to lose and wondered whether he could make a big impression by actually filling that position.

For a month and a half he promoted the position. He called old friends, made announcements at trainings and networking events. He was inundated with resumes and phone calls. He noticed that there was a buzz in the mental health community and that buzz was about him! People were grateful for the opportunity. He began e-mailing resumes of highly qualified candidates to the leadership team. And as that occurred, the CEO began talking about him in management meetings. "We need to figure out how to get this guy on our team. He doesn't even work for us and has gotten us better candidates for this position than we've ever been able to do on our own."

Thanks to my friend, the company hired a director for the position they could not fill, and they also hired a second candidate from his referral list—two high-level positions filled in a little over a month.

What happened next? I'm sure you can guess the ending. My friend received a call from the CEO thanking him and inviting him to their facility. He sat down and met the entire leadership team. The CEO asked him what he felt he could contribute to the organization. He told them all his interests and how he felt he could contribute to the company. And then the CEO said, "Great. We can create a position here that I believe will make you happy." And that's what the company did! They offered him his dream job, that he created himself, with a very nice salary increase. He has never turned back.

"WE CAN REBUILD HIM": LAUNCHING A TRANSFORMATIONAL CAMPAIGN

My friend's success story taught me many things and, more importantly, it gave me hope when I needed it most. Hopefully, you can see how he unknowingly adopted many of the principles and concepts discussed in this book. They are powerful tools that can bring you similar results.

What did he do differently? For starters, he did an amazing job of selling himself. He made himself valuable to the point where the company could no longer ignore him. He created that fundamental shift I referred to earlier in the book, a powerful move from a selling to a buying environment. In this case, my friend's approach placed him in a position of influence. The end result — the company aggressively sought him out and approached my friend with the intent of convincing him to join their company. This is a far cry from responding to want ads and praying for an interview. I had never seen anyone conduct a job search in this manner.

I must pause for a moment here to make sure you understand that this example, while unique, is entirely within your grasp. It is only unique because few people in our field are aware of the sales and marketing tools my friend used. You now hold in your hands a book containing the tools to make this scenario a reality for you!

In this chapter, I present some key job searching principles, tools, and techniques you can use to sell yourself and define a career path that matches your needs and your strengths.

GLIMPSING THE FUTURE

Today's job market is tough. We're all painfully aware of this fact. Now, more than ever, it's essential to leverage your network and to use your creativity in order to be noticed. The real-world examples discussed at the beginning of the chapter speak to the importance of selling yourself and thinking differently when conducting a job search.

One way people are beginning to make an impact with employers is through the use of new technology, most notably, social media.

Recently, I stumbled on a remarkable woman named Susan Villas Lewis. She's given new meaning to the phrase "job search." Susan reports that she was in a dip career-wise and was looking for something new and special. So she set out on her own personal career quest and identified key markets she needed to reach with impact. Susan needed to find the decision makers and the "connectors" within her industry who could help launch her in the right direction. So what did she do? She created a resume blog. Resume blogs are relatively new, and they're generating a lot of interest and discussion. Take a look at Susan's resume blog (http://main.susanhiresaboss.com/) to get an idea of just how creative and powerful they can be (see Figures 9.1).

Hi. I'm Susan.

My superpower is getting things done. It's an exceedingly rare and critical superpower.

I battle the agent of chaos. I overdeliver. I delight. I amaze.

And I'm looking for a place in need of a superhero like me.

Figure 9.1 Susan's Resume Blog Homepage
Source: From http://main.susanhiresaboss.com/ by Susan Villas Lewis. Copyright 2007. Reprinted with permisson of the author.

When you arrive at Susan's homepage it's pretty clear that this site is unique and special. Her resume blog makes her instantly memorable and has helped introduce her to some pretty amazing people within her field. This, in turn, has led to some fantastic business opportunities.

I'm not saying you should set up a site identical to Susan's. In all actuality, it wouldn't make sense to do such a thing. Her aggressive approach and unique take on things might backfire on you. But it works for her, precisely because the blog is authentically hers. It's powerful, because it is genuine and creative.

Wouldn't it be interesting if you and I decided to apply our own unique mental health twist to this new job search medium? Perhaps our resume blog would show a unique vision for mental health treatment or offer readers our own interesting insights, resources, or research. Our resume blog might even brag a little about past accomplishments, offering references and endorsements from organizational leaders.

Resume blogs can be powerful marketing vehicles that help you stand out during a competitive job search campaign. Imagine a first round of interviews where hiring managers ask candidates a series of questions based on their resumes. Let's say that instead of just sending a resume to earn your interview, you also chose to send a link to your resume blog, which was packed with useful and substantial information. This fact would lead to a much more engaging and interesting discussion during the interview. The hiring manager might ask about some of the interesting articles and position papers you wrote and posted on your site. Perhaps he or she might decide to talk about the initiative, problem solving, and creativity you clearly displayed by creating the web site in the first place!

If you're looking for impact, sometimes you've got to approach things in a different manner. Susan Villas Lewis took a chance and it paid off in a big way. What chances are you willing to take?

Exploring Your Interests and Developing a Career Plan

If you are looking for a richer and more rewarding job search experience, you must develop a written career plan. Why? Because the first shift you need to make is to think of career planning as much more than a series of steps you take to find a job that will pay the bills. It involves looking at all aspects of yourself: your likes and dislikes, your unique skills and interests, and self-destructive thought processes and behavior patterns. True career development and growth is a self-exploration process. Practical job searching skills such as interviewing techniques and resume writing are important; however, they will not necessarily help you find a career that transcends the term *work*. Yes, I understand that this is starting to sound like a self-help book, but I assure you there is true substance with this kind of approach, and it is vastly different than what 90% of people do when they are looking for employment.

Creating and using a career plan is the first step to beginning an effective job search. The pages to follow identify three key reasons why this step is so important to your success.

Reason 1: Career Plans Help You Uncover Your True Wants

We all have our own negative and self-limiting beliefs that can serve to prevent us from even entertaining certain opportunities. We might self-sabotage our ideas and interests by labeling them frivolous or unrealistic. A good career plan helps break through any resistance or negative beliefs you may have.

It gives you permission to explore your interests and helps to crystallize them through the development of goals and tasks to accomplish those goals. Career plans add balance to our wishes and desires.

Reason 2: Career Plans Bring Life to Your Goals

Want to know a 100% certainty in the area of career development? If you do not give yourself permission to nurture a particular interest or desire of yours, then it will most certainly not come to fruition. The reason why is obvious. Let's say you secretly desire to become an expert author in the area of adolescent mental health issues, but you do nothing to feed your energy around this desire. This means you don't seek out job experiences in this area to develop your skills and knowledge base, and as a result, you neither attempt to research book ideas nor ever put pen to paper. Well, chances are that you won't ever become an expert author in that field!

However, let's say you act on this desire, meaning you take steps toward a goal or goals. It may be that you simply express your specific interests and desires to others in the field, which leads to someone introducing you to a psychologist who just so happens to specialize in adolescent development research. She offers you a volunteer research position, which you happily do in the evenings and on weekends. Your work with this person helps to build your knowledge and skill in the field, and you begin to identify specific areas in the field you find fascinating. The psychologist you volunteer your time with recognizes your excitement and invites you to several national conferences where she introduces you to others who share your passion. As the years go by you gain a reputation as an expert in adolescent development, and this opens up the possibility for you to become a college professor at several leading universities. You accept a position at a school with a strong psychology department. A well-known professor at the school invites you to assist her in various research projects she is currently working on. The outcomes of these studies are published in several leading academic journals.

This is not a fictitious scenario, and the message it contains has to do with the *power of intention*. If you truly set your sights on something, then you will put your energy out into the world and ultimately create space for opportunity to present itself to you. In this case, the simple expression of interest and passion led someone on a career journey that transcended the idea of mere employment for employment sake.

Career plans help to express your intention, thereby bringing life to your goals.

Reason 3: Career Plans Keep You Focused on the Present While Being Mindful of the Future

Written career plans help to serve as an effective navigational tool. I have found that reading my career plan on a daily basis serves as a daily affirmation that helps keep me on task. It is also highly effective at keeping me focused on the present moment rather than getting completely lost in future wants and desires. This concept is critical because most people believe that career plans are entirely about future goals and accomplishments. In reality, well-done career plans provide you with specific actions and targets to work on in the here and now, while defining a long-term path you believe in and buy into.

Many people believe that writing down goals and developing a career project plan is too obvious and too simplistic. As a result, few people actually take this step. However, research shows that people who simply took the step of writing down high-level goals ended up achieving almost 80% of those goals by the end of their first year.

I encourage you to give it a try to see if it has this kind of positive impact for you.

GOAL WRITING

You can choose several approaches with regard to goal setting, and most will produce positive results for you. Some people choose to define a specific career goal, write it down, and use it as the foundation for their job search process. Others, like myself, take it another step and define a detailed plan complete with tasks and activities that support objectives, which in turn support the achievement of an overarching goal. There is no right answer as long as you are able to develop and define a career goal that is right for you.

Following is a series of goal defining steps that I use when building my own career development plan.

Step 1: Write Down Your Career Wishes

Find a quiet place to reflect, and then write down what you would like from your career in mental health. This is a difficult exercise for most people. You may find yourself trying to be practical or realistic. For now, start from a different point of reference, and write down what you truly desire! We'll get to the practical matters later.

Being practical or realistic from the start puts you face-to-face with what appear to be limited career options within the profession. You cannot go beyond some of these limits until you open yourself up to greater possibilities.

Step 2: Now Write Down What You Really Want

Now that you've made an effort to write down your career desires, take a moment to review them once again. You may find that your list remains somewhat limiting in spite of your best efforts.

Take another step toward your true career passions by, once again, writing what you would like out of a career in mental health. But this time write down what you really want!

Stretch yourself a little and give yourself permission to go beyond what your limits might appear to be. Let go of everything you have been told is impossible or unrealistic. Keep in mind that a goal should energize and excite you.

Step 3: Identify a Career Desire and Turn it into a Goal

In step three you begin the process of starting to identify a specific goal. It is here that you begin to narrow your focus.

Find the one career desire from your list that gets you most excited. (Example: I want to run a successful consulting practice.)

Now turn that statement into a specific goal. (Example: I want to run a financially prosperous and regionally recognized consulting practice targeting large to medium-sized businesses with the goal of improving organizational performance and bottom line financial results.)

When writing a goal it is good practice to develop a goal that is dynamic, meaning that it is a goal that speaks to a process rather than simply identifying something static, such as wanting to become a famous writer or own a mansion by the ocean. Dynamic goals are more empowering.

Once you create a goal you can then take steps to build a detailed plan that will include specific objectives that identify those tasks needed to achieve important targets such as the development of specific service offerings (these will include, e.g., culture/climate services, leadership training, and the development of competency-based hiring models) or the production of a business plan.

Step 4: Write Down Your Goal in the Present Tense

Career counseling experts will tell you it is important to visualize your desires and act as if they are already a reality. Putting your goal in the present tense brings new energy to it and helps to break through any resistance or doubts you may have about your goal. It brings a level of acceptance that is extremely motivating. Therefore, take your goal, and rewrite it as if it is already taking place:

"I am running a financially prosperous and regionally recognized consulting practice serving large to medium-sized businesses. Our organization has a proven track record of improving organizational performance and bottom line financial results for our clients."

These are simple steps that can help you build a solid foundation from which you can create a detailed career plan.

Another important point to note about a written career plan is that its main purpose is to build motivation and focus. I mention this because your efforts may or may not turn out exactly as planned. This is okay! Life, as we all know, is full of surprises. The intent of my goal program is to position me for success knowing that life is full of wonderful twists and turns. Your efforts may not lead to the accomplishment of a stated goal as it was initially defined, but your efforts will lead you to all kinds of unique and interesting opportunities you may not have anticipated.

I encourage you to make an effort to try this process, as it has produced tremendous results for myself and for those who have worked with me.

SELLING YOURSELF: FOUR ESSENTIAL TIPS FOR GETTING HIRED

If you're considering a job change or are just starting your mental health career, then these four tips will be invaluable to you. They'll help you build a highly effective job search campaign.

1. Your job search is not about you!

When most of us begin looking for new employment, we think about our own interests, needs, and wants first and foremost. And taking this frame of reference is a necessary and important part of any job search process. However, you must be careful not to forget the most important people in this process—the hiring organization and/or managers. The overarching reality here is that the job search process is *not* about you. Perhaps a better way to think of this is in terms of the hiring process versus the overall job search process. If you are to succeed at earning opportunities, you must focus on the needs and wants of the person who is doing the hiring. This represents a rather significant paradigm shift for many job seekers, and it is a shift that will produce great results for you.

You can use this customer-focused philosophy to produce powerful results, and there are several exercises and methods that can assist you. One of the more effective exercises you can use prior to applying for a position involves visualizing the demands currently being placed on the hiring manager. Better yet, if you have been or are currently a manager, think about a time when you needed to hire someone. What stressors were you experiencing, and what needs did you have in order to fill the job adequately? Once you have done this, take a moment and write down those ideas that come into your head. An example might look something like Table 9.1.

Table 9.1 Sample 1: Visualization Exercise

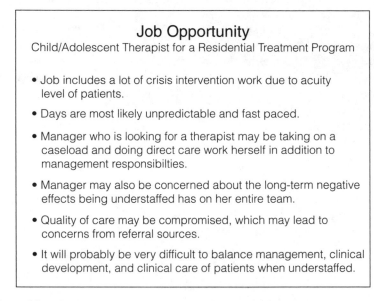

Job Opportunity
Child/Adolescent Therapist for a Residential Treatment Program

- Job includes a lot of crisis intervention work due to acuity level of patients.
- Days are most likely unpredictable and fast paced.
- Manager who is looking for a therapist may be taking on a caseload and doing direct care work herself in addition to management responsibilties.
- Manager may also be concerned about the long-term negative effects being understaffed has on her entire team.
- Quality of care may be compromised, which may lead to concerns from referral sources.
- It will probably be very difficult to balance management, clinical development, and clinical care of patients when understaffed.

Or like Table 9.2.

Table 9.2 Sample 2: Visualization Exercise

Job Opportunity
Program Director for Outpatient Group Treatment

- Leadership is temporarily filling in the gap by doing "double duty." They are concerned that this is impacting the quality of the program and morale levels of employees.
- Job included a high level of clinical skill and competence.
- Organization leaders are looking for someone who not only has strong clinical skills but also the ability to adapt quickly and to be creative in programming efforts.
- Organizational leaders want someone who is reliable, someone they do not have to micro-manage. They want someone who will take care of things and deliver a high quality product.
- Organization leaders are seeking someone who will represent the organization from a public relations standpoint. They want someone who will make an impression in the community and with referral resources.
- Organizational leaders are looking for a person who can manage and mentor others.

This simple exercise will help you to focus on the needs of the hiring manager and the organization. It also brings to mind important sales concepts I discussed in previous chapters: selling on value and trigger points.

- If you are able to identify the trigger points or pressing needs of the hiring manager, you increase the chances that a manager will contact you. In the first example, the trigger points would include the needs for continued quality of care for patients and an overworked manager who needs some relief. In the second example, organizational leaders are looking for a combination of professional skill coupled with key competencies that are not easily defined (e.g., adaptability, creativity, reliability, interpersonal skills).
- In addition, if you are able to clarify how you may be of value and how you can help solve a problem or fill a need, then you also significantly improve your chances.

After you have written some good ideas about the key stressors within the hiring organization, you can take the process a step further, and write down some key areas you can emphasize in your cover letter and on your interview. These areas will serve as the foundation for your value proposition. Some examples are as follows:

- I am highly motivated and reliable. I am able to take on challenging tasks and achieve positive results quickly. I can offer specific examples to support this fact.
- I am a quick learner and will be able to take on a caseload within a few weeks.
- I have a strong skill base giving me the ability to immediately begin running clinical groups.
- I respond well to constantly changing environments and can give detailed examples as proof.
- I am easy to work with for both managers and colleagues alike and can offer references and examples to support this fact.

By identifying these elements you are beginning the process of crafting a message you want to convey throughout the job search process. You can use these value-based messages in all aspects of the job search process. Remember, you sell yourself by thinking about the needs of your customer. In this case your customer is a potential employer.

As a hiring manager myself, I see well-intentioned and well-skilled people miss out on opportunities right from the get-go. This happens when people convey the wrong message in their cover letters or e-mail responses. Here is an example:

"I am searching for an opportunity with an up-and-coming organization where I can learn and grow in my career. I am a highly motivated individual seeking an organization where there is room for advancement."

Any variation of this is a true killer, *a surefire way to turn off the hiring manager*, because you are focusing on you rather than on the person reviewing your application. In most cases, the hiring manager who is reviewing these has limited time during the day, and yours may be one of several hundred applications on her desk. If she reads your letter and it begins with a sentence focusing on your needs, then picks up a letter from another candidate that launches right into a statement about the organization's needs, it is obvious who will win out in that scenario.

Once again, the overall message here is to focus on the needs of the customer and build a strong value message that will capture her attention and encourage her to buy your services by giving you a call to schedule an interview!

2. Think different.

There are lots of obstacles and challenges no matter what your profession. And each industry brings its own unique set of circumstances. But perhaps the biggest roadblock for many in our field is when a person cannot see beyond the more traditional opportunities available in the marketplace. I was guilty of this for years. I looked where the obvious paths were—private practice, state mental health systems, schools. Need I say more?

A year ago I heard someone say that playing it safe in mental health was a risky proposition, and I thought it offered great words of wisdom. To me it says, "Maybe the obvious career path isn't where I should be looking," or "Maybe the traditional job search process I've used for years isn't working as well as it used to."

Think about it. Less than 25% of job opportunities are advertised in the want ads, including CareerBuilder and the like. Even worse, by the time they're posted they're already old opportunities that have gone through the internal wires and networks.

I encourage you to think differently about your profession. Your success depends on it! Go ahead and take some chances, try new things, and search for unique opportunities. And if you're going to make a mistake or fail when trying, so be it! Failing means you are putting yourself out there, and sooner or later you'll win out.

Look beyond the obvious choices and pathways that the field has mapped out for you. Listen with a critical ear to those traditionalists who argue, as my graduate school professors did, that there are only a set number of ways you can work within this profession. If you do this you will find richer and more exciting opportunities out there waiting for what you bring uniquely to the table.

Approach your job search in a different way. Look in places you may not have dared explore in the past. Don't let the field define you, and you'll have a better chance of expanding your choices and opportunities.

3. Play to your strengths.

Instead of spending time trying to improve on your perceived weaknesses, why not flip it around? Take time to better understand your strengths and then build a career development plan that plays to those first and foremost.

Your skills and overall talents can be used to find opportunities in a wide variety of areas. As an example, your therapeutic skills offer a lot of value that crosses over into a variety of professional services (e.g., industrial organization psychology, business consulting, coaching, human resources, market research).

Are you new to the field, with limited experience? This isn't as big a problem as you believe it to be. When you apply for a job, focus on specific competencies that are strengths for you (e.g., creativity, adaptability, initiative, analytical thinking). Identify those attributes you believe will be valued by the hiring manager and emphasize those. I've seen many inexperienced people win out over other more qualified candidates, simply because they did a good job of showing how their problem solving skills, motivation, and adaptability from one work setting could be positively transferred to the hiring manager's work setting.

4. Be long-term focused in your efforts.

In the world of professional sales it's easy to focus your time and energy on the end of the month when you have targets to hit and commissions to earn. This approach is enticing but the better play is to build systems and networks for the long haul. The same lesson should be applied to your job search efforts. Think long-term by growing your skill set and building an ever-expanding professional network.

The message is simple. If you're in graduate school, please don't spend all your time with books and homework! Work on building your network.

If you're a seasoned professional looking for a change, then work toward achieving a balance between short-term tasks (e.g., resume writing, replying to job ads) and long-term growth (e.g., establishing strategic partnerships, building credibility).

Venture out into mental health circles, write online articles, meet new people who are doing interesting work, build strong working relationships and get noticed. Those who do this effectively will inevitably create an environment where work opportunities begin to present themselves versus having to actively seek them out.

There are a number of long-term networking and career development techniques you can adopt and I suggest using them whether you're presently searching for work or not.

The pages that follow offer you a closer look at some of these strategies.

NETWORKING SKILLS

The best job opportunities are often never advertised, and as a result, they require a very different approach if you are to uncover them with any level of success.

The most effective approach involves focusing on long-term outcomes. Why is it smarter to dedicate the majority of your time to long-term strategies rather than using more traditional short-term methods? Some of the reasons have to do with the amount of competition you will find in the marketplace and where in the job opportunity life cycle you typically find traditional job postings.

The Value of Long-Term Strategies

If you are using want ads and/or online postings to find opportunities, you are competing with a very large group of people, and you are doing so without any competitive advantage. Choosing to apply to a generic want ad is similar to choosing to sell broad-based services in the greater marketplace. Nothing has been done to narrow your focus or to identify the right prospects for you. You are responding blindly to an advertisement and positioning yourself as one of many in a vast pool of candidates. The only way you can distinguish yourself using this approach is through passive marketing vehicles such as your cover letter and resume. (Susan Villas Lewis offers us a creative exception to this rule.) In most instances, short-term job search strategies offer limited opportunities to leverage relationships or to show proven results. As a result, your success rate with this approach is greatly reduced.

One reason why a long-term approach is more effective has to do with the life cycle of job opportunities. As already noted, many of the really exciting and promising opportunities never make it to the want ads. These opportunities are often given to people who are already part of an organization's network. A hiring manager may create a new position or offer an existing one to someone they feel comfortable with or who they already know to be a good worker.

So, by the time an ad is posted, the company has most likely already gone through an internal search process. In many cases, you may be applying for a position that already has a few solid candidates who are well into the interviewing process.

As a result of these challenges, I recommend taking an approach that all successful salesmen take when they are selling their services and/or products. That approach is a long-term, value-based and relationship-centered one. It's a process you should be following even when you are not looking for employment. If you take the time to focus on meeting the needs of others and work on building relationships, opportunities will begin to present themselves to you.

Informational Interviewing

Informational Interviewing is an excellent job search approach you can use to effectively build your network and uncover hidden opportunities. In my experiences, it is *the* most effective job search approach available to you and it's a process you should be following even when you're not actively looking for employment.

In summary, it involves contacting leaders within your industry and asking them if you can meet to learn more about the work they do. The idea is to build a knowledge base that will help you decide where you would like to focus your career development efforts and to understand what skills and competencies are essential if you are to be successful. It's a great way to grow professionally while building a strong network at the same time. You will also find that people are much more approachable when you use this method as opposed to calling for employment. People, for the most part, enjoy helping others and imparting wisdom, so do not be shy about asking. More often than not, you will be rewarded with face-to-face meetings with top level professionals you would not otherwise have a chance to meet.

The main steps outlining the informational interviewing process are as follows.

Step 1: Identify a Group of Individuals and Organizations in Your Field to Contact

Research your areas of interest and find out who is doing that kind of work nearby. Be creative and really think about those areas you've always found interesting but never thought were realistic.

I worked with one mental health professional who was interested in leadership and work climate issues but she never figured there would be opportunities for her based on her psychology background and mental health experience. However, when she researched this area she found some interesting professionals in human resources and management consulting with backgrounds similar to hers. She scheduled some meetings and was able to talk with and learn from many of these people. She uncovered a whole new area where her counseling skills were being used and she learned what path she needed to take in order to be considered for some of these opportunities.

Step 2: Develop a Short Commercial about Why You are Calling

Once you have a list of some interesting people you'd like to call, work on a brief commercial about why you are calling. It should go something like this:

> "Hello, my name is Joe Smith. I'm a vocational counselor with Organization Y. I'm interested in the addiction field, and I heard you give a talk on the recovery group process for adolescents a few months ago. I was wondering if I could meet with you briefly to learn more about the work you do so I could begin taking steps to enter the addiction treatment field."

One key point to make here is that you *do not* want to ask for a job when you are initially contacting people. Be clear that you're doing research to determine where you want to go in your career.

Your goal when you call is to simply get an appointment to meet, not to earn a job interview.

Step 3: Ask Good Questions

Being prepared, showing that you value the other person's time is an excellent way to make an impression. You'd be surprised how rarely this takes place.

Let's say you have an informational interview coming up with a clinician who has done a fair amount of research on addictions treatment. Which question do you think would make a bigger impression?

> "Thanks for meeting with me. I know you're well known for your work pertaining to victimization and PTSD in substance abusers. I have a lot of interest in that area and was wondering if you could tell me what led you in that direction in terms of your career."

or

> "Thanks for meeting with me, I was hoping you could tell me what it is you do and how you got to this point."

Have several good questions you can ask that show you have put a lot of thought into this process. The quality of your questions will be a distinguishing factor for you.

Step 4: Have Your Resume in Tip-Top Shape

Bring your resume with you because you never know when you might need it. The people you meet will be assessing you and forming their own impressions. They will be thinking, *"Where might this person fit now or down the road in my organization?"*

Step 5: Make a Positive Impression

Okay, I know this sounds painfully obvious but it needs to be emphasized. Take advantage of the time someone has been willing to give you! Remember, while you're not directly asking for a job, you are being interviewed. Be prepared to make a positive impression—people will be assessing you, and it may lead to a job today, tomorrow, or down the road.

I know several people who went into informational interviews and came out that day with a new job! The person you are meeting might think of someone they know who is hiring, and they may choose to refer you to him. In other instances, they may be compelled to offer you an opportunity within their department or on their team.

The lists of possibilities is endless, and it all starts with getting your foot in the door so you can build your network.

Step 6: Always Leave with Something

Step six adopts a classic best practice sales principle. Be sure you ask the person you are meeting if she can recommend other people in the field to talk with or if she knows of any professional development community events. The idea is to walk away with ever-expanding opportunities you can explore.

I am a big supporter and proponent of the informational interviewing process. Give it a try and see what kind of positive results it produces for you!

Behavioral Event Interviewing

The interview process today often consists of highly sophisticated assessment tools and research-based applications hiring managers use to predict the level of success a candidate might offer. One common approach used is called behavioral event interviewing. This approach to interviewing takes the position that specific competencies and characteristics are essential to success in the workplace. In many instances, these characteristics outweigh skills and experience.

As a hiring manager myself, I discovered that the people who were most successful in my organization were those who tended to have a certain set of characteristics that transcended years of experience and specific skill sets. Industrial organizational psychologists support this assumption. Their research shows that skills and formal education are simply a baseline component of success. In reality, each position has a core set of competencies that distinguish the successful from the not so successful. And if an organization is able to identify those competencies most critical to their line of business and work culture, they can search for candidates who possess these competencies and ultimately find the best candidates.

So what are competencies? Some good examples are as follows:

- Leadership
- Analytical thinking
- Initiative
- Interpersonal skills
- Creativity
- Motivation
- Problem solving
- Adaptability
- Emotional control
- Teamwork

These are just a few examples of competencies and the overall model is important for you to understand, because it can help you shine in an interview.

If hiring managers present a scenario asking you to tell them about a time when you had to solve a difficult problem, you can assume they are looking for and assessing your level of problem solving abilities. This approach has proven to be extremely effective, and one reason why is that it gets to the essential success factors for a job. Many people can present well in an interview or look fantastic on paper. However, managers can get a real look at a candidate's potential by examining real-world situations. Many organizations hire human resource consulting firms who help define competency models that are used as the main component of an organization's hiring process. These can be very sophisticated models based on vast amounts of data to improve validity and reliability. Take adaptability as an example. A company may have adaptability listed as a critical success factor and within the adaptability competency they might have a rating system to help managers determine how sophisticated a candidate is with regard to that specific competency. The more sophisticated the level of adaptability, the higher the score.

Tables 9.3 and 9.4 provide examples of how one organization uses the competencies **adaptability** and **motivation** to assess candidates.

One great way to make an impression during an interview is to emphasize key competencies you believe you possess and give specific examples

Table 9.3 *Competency Model: Sample 1*

Adaptability

Level 1: Employee is able to put a task on hold in order to focus on a new task/demand.

Level 2: Employee demonstrates an ability to work in a constantly changing environment whereby he or she may be asked to work on an issue with accounting and then brainstrom with clinicians about treatment programming.

Level 3: Employee, faced with multiple demands, identifies a unique approach and solutions so that all tasks are completed successfully. This might include negotiating and partnering with other departments and/or individuals. Additional resources that are managed by the employee help to ensure work is being completed while freeing up his or her time to work on other activities.

Table 9.4 *Competency Model: Sample 2*

Motivation

Level 1: Employee takes direction well, listens intently to directives, and is driven to accomplish the given task to its fulltest.

Level 2: Employee is highly self-motivated and is able to infer what is required to solve a problem or complere a task. He or she puts a significant amount of time and energy into accomplishing the task, even when he or she is not asked to do so directly.

Level 3: Employee is willing to take on complex and difficult tasks. He or she shows an impressive ability to understand what work needs to be done without being given clear direction. In addition, the employee is rarely dissuaded, and when faced with obstacles, he or she takes the time to figure out alternative solutions until the work is successfully completed.

---

throughout the interview process. If you work well in teams or if you have great analytical skills, find opportunities to provide examples.

Keep in mind that competencies often win out over work experience and skill. How? Well, let's say you interview a highly skilled person with a significant amount of job experience. The only issue is that he comes across as a bit arrogant, and you begin wondering if he might be difficult to work with and to manage. Days later you interview a less experienced person who offers you great work examples that show an ability to work well in teams and a proven track record in a constantly changing work environment. Who would you choose if you were the hiring manager?

Keep competencies in mind as you go through the hiring process!

The job search process has gone through significant change and will continue to do so in the years to come. The sales and marketing concepts discussed in this chapter and throughout the book represent new and innovative approaches that will serve you well in your search.

And as you go through the day-to-day process of finding work, always remember these principles and use them to sell yourself in state-of-the-art fashion!

Be unique in your approach, focus on the needs of others, build strong relationships, and expand your skill and knowledge base.

In the end, these ideals will lead you on a path to new opportunities in the field.

SUMMARY

- A written and detailed plan is an essential component for building career success.
- A career plan offers three main benefits: (1) It uncovers your true wants; (2) it builds motivation and a level of activity that allow opportunity to find you; (3) it keeps focus on the present while being mindful of the future.
- When conducting your job search, take the position that your search is not about your needs but about those of the potential employer. Demonstrate how you can solve a problem for the company or meet its needs, and you will greatly improve your chances of being hired.
- Be creative and memorable in your job search efforts. Resume blogs are one option that can have a big impact. Revisit the section on resume

blogs to learn more about what they are all about and how they can work for you.

- Informational interviewing is one of the most powerful job search tools and will help you uncover excellent opportunities that are never advertised.
- Behavioral event interviewing is becoming a more common approach adopted by hiring managers. It is designed to identify competencies that are critical to success. Examples of competencies are: analytical skills, creativity, initiative, and teamwork.

CHAPTER TEN

Build a Better Web site
Web Site Essentials for Mental Health Professionals

More and more mental health professionals have a web site or are thinking seriously about creating one. And it's exciting to see your name out there in lights for the entire world to see! So you build "About Us" pages, talk about your education and credentials, briefly discuss your services, and offer a "Contact Us" page. Others will choose to go even farther and write several paragraphs about their psychotherapeutic model or they may include a comprehensive list of facts about various mental health disorders. And while information is nice to include, too much information (especially information about you) can be counterproductive. It's not uncommon for people to lose sight of the fact that a web page is most effective when it is treated as a step in the process. Web pages are, in essence, marketing tools designed to get viewers from point A to point B. Understanding this fact can go a long way to ensuring you are getting the most out of your site.

When people visit a web site they look at what the site has to offer and then they take some sort of action. Here are a few things web visitors might do when they visit your site.

- They browse the site quickly, and if it's not interesting to them they move on to another web site.
- They might find interesting information on a web page they are viewing, and as a result, they click and go somewhere else on the web site (preferably to someplace that you want them to go!).
- They come to a site and choose to "opt-in," meaning they like what the site offers and are presented with a way that they can stay in touch and receive more information from the web site.

- If given the opportunity, they might purchase something that is offered on the web site.
- They contact the owner of the web site by phone or e-mail (perhaps to set an appointment).
- They tell a friend or friends about the site.

Creating a web site can be a frustrating process and there are a lot of ways in which you can make life difficult for yourself by creating a site that simply does not benefit you. You can, for example, create a lot of problems for yourself if you choose to cut corners in the development process. However, hiring someone to build a web site for you does not necessarily mean that success is assured. All kinds of people might claim that they can help you. Many cannot. And if you choose the wrong person it can lead to all kinds of problems, not the least of which would be a marketing message and image that hinders rather than helps.

This chapter offers important information about good web design. In order to accomplish this goal I felt it was important to have input from someone who was in the web design field. The pages to follow include a series of questions and answers from an interview with a top-notch web developer. His answers should help you to better understand what it takes to create a web site that will effectively market you and your practice.

WEB DESIGN QUESTIONS AND ANSWERS

The following questions were presented to and answered by Richard Powell, a well-respected and experienced web designer. Mr. Powell is the founder of the web development company Samedis Design (samedis.com). After studying photography in college and working for several years as a web designer for a large global company, Richard moved to Chapel Hill, North Carolina and started working directly with clients as Samedis Design. He has designed and built web sites and web applications for local, national, and international clients. He works with a wide variety of clients that include financial services firms, educational institutions, medical practices, artists, and mental health professionals. Richard enjoys getting to know the businesses he works with and the challenges of bringing their varied visions to the Web.

Would you give us three or four key design elements that are critical to the development of a good web site?

I think the primary purpose of design on a web site is to support a business's online goals. For some sites, this might mean paying close attention to the typography and readability so that the visitor can read the content without being distracted by other elements. For other sites, this might mean creating a Wow! moment when the visitor first arrives at the page, then quickly guiding their eye to a prominent call to action. Other web sites might be deep and full of useful information, but require a solidly thought out and easy to use navigation scheme to ensure the visitor is able to find exactly what they are looking for. These things are important to all sites, but it's important to identify the main goals of the web site and to bring the design to bear on strongly supporting those particular goals.

What is essential for a service-based business in terms of a Web presence and subsequent design?

For many small service-based businesses, there may not exist the budget to build out a comprehensive web site detailing absolutely everything about their business and to preemptively answer every question that a visitor might have for them. In those cases, the goal of the site is nearly always to prompt the visitor to contact them. The web site should make this as easy as possible, with a phone number posted prominently on the homepage and either an e-mail address or contact form easily available on the site. This is also true for larger businesses; however, they may have the ability to provide more information on the site and to get visitors the answers they need without needing to phone or e-mail.

The design of the web site, as with all design materials for the business, should express the feeling and mood of the company. Is it warm, personal, and welcoming, or a little more distant and corporate? Should it be bright and youthful, or restrained and moderate? When speaking with a web designer, it's important to have a conversation about the values and style of the business and how that can be translated to the web site.

How do I make my web site more than just "brochure ware"?

While a simple Web presence is a great way to get started, there are many opportunities now to go beyond the basic brochure-style website. A blog…is an excellent means for adding a more personal voice to your web site and to write on topics of interest relating to your business. Blogs often allow visitors to comment on your posts to begin a two-way dialog, allowing your visitors to communicate with you, not just the other way around. If you find that you are getting a lot of comments and your visitors are able to support each other, rather than relying on you to answer every comment, a great next step would be to integrate a discussion forum.

As tools and services on the Web continue to develop, it's becoming easier and cheaper to add surveys, e-commerce, video, e-mail newsletters, and even social networking to your site. A danger nowadays is to add a lot of bells and whistles to the web site that become a distraction, rather than a support, to the core goals of the web site. It's always crucial to review what those goals are and to evaluate how to best support them.

What are some of the most common mistakes you see people make with their web sites?

A lot of mistakes that I see are really prompted by the best of intentions. Web site owners may have heard that it's important for search engines to have lots of pages of content stuffed with keywords and so wind up writing their site for Google, not for their visitors. Similarly, they may keep adding more and more pages of content without realizing that their navigation system can't keep up and it actually makes it harder for visitors to find what they need. I've also seen a lot of people get too caught up in the "Wow" factor of the site, adding video, animation and graphics, but then hiding the phone number in small text on the footer of a hard to find contact page.

An important question when working on a web site is "What are my visitors looking for? Will this help them find it?"

What questions should I ask a web developer when I am looking to find the right company?

My first recommendation, before even speaking with a web designer or developer, would be to review their portfolio. Click through web sites that they've created in the past and gauge for you how successful they are. This will also help you in a conversation with them as you'll be able to discuss their prior work and how it relates to your proposed project, giving you both a common reference.

More important, I feel, than what specific questions you ask, is how your web designer, developer or web company answers them. A successful web site is one that grows and changes with the business and so you're not hiring someone to do a one-off job, but looking to establish a relationship. Your web designer should be able to answer your questions well and make you feel comfortable asking them! They should be able to discuss your overall strategy moving forward and how they will be able to support your business and your web site as it changes and evolves.

The final thing I would recommend is to be upfront with budgetary needs and possible constraints. Working with clients, I find it much easier to have a good idea of what my client is able to put into a project, rather than guessing at a figure. Among other things, it helps me to understand if I'm able to provide a fully bespoke solution or if I will need to work with more off the shelf products, or even if I'm not the right person for the job. There are many different ways to build a successful web site and being able to discuss these and the possible constraints with your web designer is very important.

What warning signs are there that would suggest I avoid working with a web company?

The first is simply comfort level, as discussed above. You shouldn't have to have a full understanding of how a web site works in order to work with a web company. If you're overwhelmed by "techno speak" and aren't fully understanding of certain aspects of the site or project, it may not be the right company for you. Building a web site involves technical expertise, so your web company should be proficient in that, but it also involves design and understanding of how a human will interact with it.

A strong warning sign is if your web company is too involved with the technical aspects rather than the human aspects of your web site.

Would you offer some information on the psychology of the Web, meaning how a user surfs the Web and views your site?

This is quite a large topic and so I won't attempt to cover it all here! (For more information, search "psychology of web design" or something similar and you should find plenty to read.) Below are a couple of key thoughts however that are good to keep in mind when designing a site.

First, when dealing with user interfaces there seems to be a rough limit of around seven items that humans can keep in memory at one time. This is of particular use to know when designing the navigation of your web site. If you have a navigation system with 15 different menu options, then visitors to your site will have a harder time sorting through them and navigating around the site. Instead, group them into five to seven categories and simplify the navigation scheme. Visitors will have a much easier time remembering your menu and moving around your site.

The other observation relates to reading content on web sites. People reading web sites tend to skim far more than they do when reading printed materials. As it's so easy to click away to another web site, visitors will skim down the page to see if it provides the information they're looking for before actually reading it word for word. This isn't necessarily the case with news stories or blog posts where the visitor is explicitly coming to the site to read the content, but upon their first encounter with your site, it is important to recognize this. In understanding this fact, you can better organize your content with an emphasis on headlines, bullet points, callout text and brief summaries at the top of the page. That will help your visitors to get the most out of your content in a quick period of time. Once you have them hooked, it's more likely that they'll pause and read further into your web site content.

It should also be noted that search engines pay particular attention to text in headers, links, bold text, bullets, etc. as they are a good indicator for the overall content of the page.

Everyone is always talking about SEO (Search Engine Optimization). How can I get higher up on search lists?

This is another great question that entire books have been written about and businesses have been built to answer this one question!

I find the best way to understand SEO is in terms of a "real world" analogy: imagine that you're starting a retail business just off of Main Street. You want to get the word out to everyone so that they'll come to your store and, while you've put out advertisements in the paper, you know that the best advertising comes from word of mouth. Similarly, on the web, you can place ads on Google or other sites, but what you really want is to be found "organically" in search engine results as that costs a lot less and is generally more trusted. As with the real world store, you need to make sure that your web site is "optimized" inside so that it's clear what your business is about. A store might post signs and displays with the different items for sale; your web site will need to have headings, links, bullets that include the keywords describing your business.

But the real goal is to get people to talk about your store. In our real world scenario, people will recommend your store to a friend. On the Web, that's achieved with a link to your site. You want to get as many people talking as possible, or as many people linking to your site as you can. As in the real world, certain people's opinions carry more weight than others. So while it can't hurt that the mailman is recommending you, if you sell women's clothes, a link from a noted fashion editor would be far more beneficial.

So there are really two key elements—internally optimizing your web site by writing quality content, and ensuring that the keywords that describe your business are used in page titles, headers, etc. and to get people linking to you. Great ways to get people linking to you are by posting your site in appropriate industry and local directories, commenting on related blogs, swapping links with other professionals, and traditional PR techniques to notify people of your site.

There's no real " magic bullet" in SEO, and if someone offers you a way to get to the top of Google within a few days, then it's likely that they're doing something unscrupulous. Google and other search engines do crack down and punish web sites that try to unfairly game the system, so it's best to approach SEO with an eye to long-term results.

———

I want to stress that developing an effective web site should be considered as an important part of your overall marketing strategy and plan. If your site is done well it will help grow your business.

Nowadays, when people are looking for mental health services they use the Internet as a research tool to learn more about you and your services. Even if you come highly recommended, people will most likely do additional research, and part of their efforts may involve an Internet search. If you don't have a web site, they'll want to know why. And if you do have a web site, ask yourself what potential clients will experience when they visit. A web site can help explain your clinical approach and your level of expertise. In addition, your web site has an overall structure, look, and feel that will impact people on an emotional level. If the emotional response is a positive one, your chances of earning their business increase significantly.

If you don't have a web site yet, take some time to research web design options and see which approach would best meet your needs and your professional goals. And if you already have a web site, review it with a critical eye and see where you can make improvements and changes that will have a positive impact for you and your business.

SUMMARY

- Web pages are, in essence, marketing tools designed to get viewers from point A to point B.
- It's important to identify the main goals of the web site and to ensure they strongly support your overall business goals.
- When speaking with a web designer, it's important to have a conversation about the values and style of the business and how that can be translated to the web site.
- A blog is an excellent means for adding a more personal voice to your web site and to write on topics of interest relating to your business. Blogs often allow visitors to comment on your posts to begin a two-way dialog, allowing your visitors to communicate with you, not just the other way around.
- A good first step when looking for a web designer is to review his or her portfolios. Click through web sites that they've created in the past and determine how successful you believe they are.
- Your web designer should be able to answer your questions well and make you feel comfortable asking them! He or she should be able to discuss your overall strategy moving forward and describe how he or she will be able to support your business and your web site as it changes and evolves.

CHAPTER ELEVEN

Service Trends within Our Changing Industry

The overall review presented in this chapter focuses on interesting trends occurring right now within the mental health profession. My hope is that this review will help generate excitement and energy for you by creating an environment of creative introspection. You may find some of these trends intriguing and worth a closer look. Others may not be of any interest whatsoever.

In my opinion, what is most important is the simple act of engaging in the process itself. When you take a moment to understand the current trends and changes within your industry you keep yourself open to possibility.

Some of the trends we will explore are as follows.

- Virtual communities and Web seminars
- The coaching profession
- Online psychotherapy
- Online training

With an eye toward new possibility and opportunity, let's take a closer look and see if any of these trends excite or interest you.

THE INTERNET AND THE WINDOW OF OPPORTUNITY

Today's technological advances have led to a dramatic shift in how business is done and offer all of us an opportunity to move beyond traditional boundaries to reach more diverse audiences.

The Internet alone has led to a mass decentralization of power that has brought about incredible, and, at times, seemingly limitless opportunity.

It is an attractive medium for many reasons:

- **The variety of messaging capabilities**: Video, audio, community forums, blogs, Web seminars. The list continues to grow in terms of the type and complexity of messages one can use to reach others. Within this realm are vast opportunities to reach consumers and to build an effective self-marketing plan.
- **Building your own presence on the Web**: Unlike television or radio, anyone can have a web site and gain a presence on the Web with minimal effort and investment.
- **Power to the user**: At present, there is limited control and regulation of the Web. As a result, the power to accomplish many business activities and to reach others has shifted from the few to the many.
- **Access to knowledge and information**: The Internet offers people a vehicle for researching, communicating, and dispersing information at a level never before seen in our history.

What might this mean for you? Certainly tremendous opportunity for growing your practice, selling and marketing your services, communicating your expertise, and even defining new service offerings that leverage the Internet and reach a different client base.

Virtual Communities: Client Conversations on the Internet

One example of this trend at a local level involves a woman who started a Yahoo! group for caregivers of children with autism. Within six months her group grew exponentially. Mental health practitioners offered it as a resource, and families spoke about it to others within their community. The group provided an online forum where people could ask questions, learn about valuable resources, and build relationships with others who could empathize with their situation. It was particularly powerful with parents who were feeling isolated and were coming to terms with their child's disability. This online community provided a highly supportive and informative environment that had not existed prior to the formation of this social network. Without it, families simply had no options other than receiving guidance and suggestions from family physicians or mental health practitioners.

Two interesting social networking groups available today are www.webtribes.com and www.realmentalhealth.com. Both are social networking sites focusing on mental health and wellness. They represent communities for people suffering from any number of psychiatric conditions, and they give users the ability to interact with other people in a variety of ways. Participants can create their own free account, which gives them the ability to build their own webpage on the site. They can participate in video- and audio-based chat rooms that are organized by specific topic such as depression, bipolar disorder, or schizophrenia. There are message boards, newsletters, and an extensive list of support groups for site users.

One of the reasons why online support communities are so powerful is the fact that they are easy to approach anonymously. This anonymity factor is a powerful draw for many who are in crisis and for those who might not reach out otherwise, were it not for the availability of these support groups. The presence of these networking sites provides some interesting opportunities and challenges for the mental health professional.

For starters, online communities can be an excellent entry point for people to eventually seek treatment. It is an especially promising referral source for those clinicians who are able to gain a presence within these communities. We all know that the decision to seek treatment can be a long and convoluted process. With the social network model, many people feel safe seeking help. As a result, clinicians are able to reach a captive audience of people who already recognize they need help, and therefore, may be more receptive to taking the next logical step in the treatment process. On the other hand, practitioners also must be aware that the effectiveness and growing popularity of these communities may reduce the need and/or use of more traditional and professional models of treatment. This trend is definitely worth exploring and ripe with opportunity!

Web Seminars (Webinars)

Not too long ago, Oprah Winfrey offered a free 10-week web seminar with spiritual guru and author Eckhart Tolle. The webinar was held every Monday evening for 10 weeks. What is important to note about this hallmark event, regardless of whether you are an Oprah fan, is the fact that together they held an interactive educational program on a global scale. Participants entered a virtual learning environment where they could access workbooks and course material, post questions, and view real-time discussions and presentations by Eckhart Tolle. Not impressed so far? How about the fact that they had over 700,000 participants each week from 139 countries!

This single event demonstrated the power of web seminars and introduced a mass audience to this technology. No longer is it simply a tool for facilitating virtual business meetings. It has become an effective vehicle for communicating a message, building awareness and buy-in about a particular topic, and offering an interactive educational experience.

Web seminars, as part of the rising social nature of the web, will become more and more prominent in our near future. Larger behavioral health care organizations and practitioners alike will want to keep an eye on this model and think about how it might be useful in their profession.

The Rise of Professional Coaching

In early 2007, I was speaking with a friend who told me he had attended a relationship workshop he found to be very informative and helpful for both him and his wife. Naturally, I assumed it was either a psychologist, marriage and family therapist, professional counselor, or clinical social worker facilitating the program. Since I was in the field and felt I had a good handle on the marketplace, I assumed I would know the clinician. When I asked the person's name, I did not recognize it. I asked my friend if the person was a therapist, and he nodded his head in acknowledgment. Since I did not know this person, I looked her up and realized she was not a clinician but a relationship coach.

Several points from this conversation are worth noting. One is the fact that there are people in your community providing a variety of individual and group services who are *not* mental health professionals in the traditional sense. The second point is that many of the people offering these services are very good at what they do. The third is that they are business savvy. They know how to market their services and how to speak to consumers. Finally, the reality is that most people outside of mental health are not aware of the distinction between a mental health clinician and a relationship coach. They see them as interchangeable, as one and the same. Let's briefly take a look at these important points since they speak to a phenomenon that will have more and more of an effect on the mental health profession as a whole.

a. Coaches and Consultants

Coaching is growing at an international level, and these professionals are involved in numerous areas that overlap with mental health services. Some of these areas include career counseling, relationship counseling, leadership counseling, life change consulting, business consulting, and grief counseling. They have done an excellent job of penetrating highly lucrative markets such as Fortune 500 companies, CEO-level executives, schools, and high-end communities. In the past there was a stigma associated with this profession. However, the stigma has lessened considerably, and in many parts of the world it is virtually nonexistent. In addition, many of these programs and service offerings are of very high quality. They are well researched, innovative, and highly structured. I recently attended a workshop delivered by a life coach who worked with people going through significant life changes, including death of a loved one, life-threatening illness, divorce, career change, unemployment, or any number of other things. The program was well-defined, unique, and utilized both clinical and coaching principles. It was a very effective program!

b. Marketing and Sales Savvy

Adding to the dilemma for mental health practitioners is the fact that many coaches are experienced in all areas of business. They know how to uncover needs and opportunities and then design and market programs that will speak to potential consumers. In many ways they are ahead of the curve in terms of sales and marketing principles. They are also able to leverage technology to improve their reach and expand their presence in the market.

Another interesting aspect of life coaches is that they are very specific with regard to their target audience, and as a result, they craft their message accordingly. These are important lessons to be aware of as you move forward in your career. Being clear as to whom you are offering services to will help you to use your time wisely when it comes to marketing and selling. The good news is that you can learn a lot researching some of these professionals and taking a look at what they do effectively and not so effectively.

Want some good examples of what I am talking about when I refer to life coaches?

Take a look at Martha Beck. Martha is a life coach who gives us a good example of how professional coaches are taking a piece of the market away from mental health professionals. You can learn more about her at www.marthabeck.com. She has written several books and offers individual coaching sessions, teleseminars and much more. All her services are designed to help people change their lives, and her approach is engaging, well designed, and well received by people looking for help.

Another site that will give you an idea of the power and scope life coaches and consultants offer is www.simpleology.com. This is a concept offered by marketing expert Mark Joyner. He would not necessarily consider himself a life coach, however, his Simpleology program is based on scientific and behavioral research and is designed to help people manage and make sense of their hectic lives. It proposes to offer solutions that will increase productivity and peace of mind. In addition, he leverages the power of the Internet to reach a broad audience by offering a sophisticated learning platform complete with free modules and software tools designed to help you prioritize and manage daily tasks and goals. His program should give mental health professionals a much better picture of the kinds of programs and service offerings behavioral healthcare practitioners can develop and promote.

ONLINE PSYCHOTHERAPY

Online counseling and psychotherapy is slowly becoming a more and more realistic option for people in need of psychological help and guidance. This model has certainly received its fair share of criticism, especially from the mental health community at large. It has its limitations, no doubt, which I will not go into here. But technology is catching up with this model as high-speed wireless Internet access, video/audio streaming, and webcam capabilities become commonplace. In many instances, a session between a therapist and a patient in two different locations can be bridged quite effectively with the right technological specifications.

In the world of academia, we are seeing an increase in interest along with research in the area of online psychotherapy. One interesting resource worth a look comes from psychologist John Suler, PhD, of Rider University. In his prophetic article on "The Future of Online Psychotherapy and Clinical Work" published in the *Journal of Applied Psychoanalytic Studies* (2001), he predicts there will eventually be online psychotherapy specialists for each of the different types of online clinical models and formats.

His discussion also offers a good model for understanding the progression of online counseling to date. Dr. Suler begins with a discussion of online psychotherapy that utilizes e-mail as the primary mode of interaction. He eventually brings us to the next stage in the development of online psychotherapy, which uses a more synchronous model *(a type of two-way communication with virtually no time delay, allowing participants to respond in real time)* such as chat therapy, where there is real-time text-based interaction between client and therapist. Finally, he speaks of present day online therapy using a synchronous video-based format whereby the client and therapist talk to and see one another in real time via the Internet.

More and more practitioners are taking this mode of service delivery seriously in spite of some limitations that exist. If we are to look at this phenomenon from a business opportunity standpoint, we see that there will be demand beyond regional borders for those clinicians who position themselves effectively and build a certain level of credibility in the field. It is not hard to imagine a scenario involving an individual who suffers from a specific and/or unique psychological problem. This person chooses to research the perceived problem/symptoms on the Internet and finds an expert in that subject that he or she chooses to seek services from regardless of the professional's location. A practitioner who has marketed himself or herself effectively and has utilized today's technology to offer something of value to others beyond traditional face-to-face psychotherapy will have a competitive advantage in that marketplace.

Dr. Suler piques the reader's interest even further with a discussion about the ability of the Internet to create imagery and multimedia environments that can be used in clinical interventions. Virtual realities are already being used in exposure therapy and relaxation procedures. He wonders if there might also be a place for virtual reality in trauma work, behavioral modeling, and role-playing, to name a few. If you would like more information about this topic I suggest you look at Dr. Suler's online book, *The Psychology of Cyberspace*, at http://www-usr.rider.edu/~suler/psycyber/psycyber.html

We are already seeing growth in this area, as Dr. Suler predicted. Take a look at the work being done at a company called InWorld Solutions™ — www.InWorldSolutions.com. InWorld Solutions began offering its software, InWorld, in October 2009. It is the first Internet-based virtual environment designed specifically for behavioral health care. It uses emerging technology and cognitive behavior therapy principles to create virtual environments that become a part of the overall clinical treatment process. It was initially used for troubled teens in residential settings and combined role-play computer generated environments with talk therapy. Les Paschall, the co-founder of InWorld Solutions, issued a press release to help explain the company's vision.

"InWorld is designed to manage a wide range of disorders, and we're seeing unprecedented levels of engagement and participation in our first use with clients who suffer from oppositional defiance disorder, attention deficit hyperactivity disorder, and post-traumatic stress disorder, as well as patients dealing with issues of anger management and substance abuse."

These are interesting times indeed!

I encourage you to stretch your views, concepts, and ideas about the clinical process and begin seeing what may lie ahead in the future as both a challenge and opportunity. One of those opportunities will be online psychotherapy in its many variations and specialties.

ONLINE TREATMENT PROGRAMS

Another interesting area arising within the industry is the online treatment program. This model goes beyond individual psychotherapy and offers a comprehensive approach to treatment that may include group work, interactive exercises, use of clinical tools, use of assessment applications, and aftercare programming.

An example of this kind of approach is being pioneered by an organization known as eGetGoing, Inc. This organization offers a substance abuse treatment program for adults ages 18 and older using live video and audio technology that simulate a traditional treatment model based on the 12-step principles. Participants become part of an online treatment group that takes place over the course of several months. eGetGoing uses a highly structured and empirically based treatment model and provides each participant with a headset and microphone in order to interact with a group of up to 10 participants. A counselor facilitates each group, and participants also receive individual consultations as needed. In addition, eGetGoing, Inc. offers an aftercare program for successful graduates in an effort to support former participants who are out in the community. This also gives them the ability to track outcomes and to identify risk factors following treatment.

This type of model is a big undertaking and, at present, it is still in its infancy stage. However, adventurous organizations like egetGoing, Inc. are making a valiant effort to offer this solution as an alternative to traditional treatment. It is an exciting area to explore in the near future as technology offers clinicians an opportunity to push the envelope and explore use of this format in other areas of treatment. This model also has promise from a business perspective in that it offers potential clients a solid value proposition that may distinguish itself from its more traditional competitors. Some of the key values to potential consumers are ease of access and approachability, confidentiality, and overall convenience in a fast-paced world. Some, however, may argue that this also offers clients an opportunity to resist treatment in a subtle way by choosing a treatment alternative that might require less commitment. Regardless of this argument, people who are in need of treatment services may in the future find themselves more willing to seek treatment through the Internet. Perhaps this will serve as an entry point for longer-term treatment. People who are unsure of the need for treatment may choose to try an online option as a way to test the waters. A bigger question will be whether or not this model will go beyond being a mere entry point and serve as a viable option to a more traditional treatment model.

If you would like more information about this model, I suggest taking a look at the EgetGoing website: www.egetgoing.com.

ONLINE TRAINING: A UNIQUE WAY TO PROMOTE YOUR SERVICES

Looking for ways to share your expertise and promote your services beyond traditional training opportunities? E-learning is fast becoming a powerful medium for building credibility and expanding one's reach at a national and international level. Online learning has also become an important vehicle for employee assistance programs and other practitioners who are seeking a presence within the corporate world. It allows you the ability to offer significant value to employees and managers using a platform they are familiar with and comfortable using.

Some mental health e-learning providers to explore are:

www.ceu4u.com

www.phoenix.edu (This site will also offer paid opportunities to teach online classes.)

www.psybc.com

www.speedyceus.com

In many instances, you can post your coursework with one of these sites or any other existing training platform. Another option is to simply create your own personal online training platform. I have seen business savvy clinicians use this as an extension of clinical services they offer other practitioners and potential clients. How can you possibly do this without paying a pretty penny? Easy! In today's world there are several free open source learning management systems available to you. These systems allow you to quickly and easily create your own e-learning courses and programs.

Some open source platforms to explore are:

www.atutor.ca

www.claroline.net

www.moodle.org

Professional associations have also gotten into the e-learning game and offer numerous courses for members. Take a look at the American Counseling Association's efforts in this regard at www.counseling.org. You'll find a link to online learning under their Resources tab. Another powerful way to expand your reach and build credibility within the profession is to develop an online course that is approved and posted on a national association web site. This is a great marketing strategy for you.

SUMMARY

- Online psychotherapy and web-based training are becoming more acceptable options for consumers. Take time to learn about each, as they can be both a challenge and opportunity depending on how you approach their existence.
- The evolving social aspects of the Internet have brought about virtual communities where people obtain information and support from one another. Ignore or discount their impact and you will lose clients to these communities. Embrace them and identify ways to leverage their existence, and you will be rewarded.
- Professional coaching is receiving more and more attention, interest, and credibility. Understand its role in your market and learn from some of the things coaches do very well in the areas of marketing and service delivery.

CHAPTER TWELVE

Conclusion

The mental health profession offers a multitude of exciting, enriching, and rewarding opportunities. The possibilities for success are numerous regardless of what you hear or in spite of your past and present experiences. Some of the keys to overcoming obstacles and uncovering opportunity within the profession can be found in the many sales and marketing principles discussed in this book. These tools and techniques will help add to your existing skill set and will change the way you operate within the field so you can build even greater success.

I have talked at length about financial rewards, career growth, and competing successfully in the profession throughout this book. I realize that, on the surface, this overall message runs counter to the values and tenets within the field, however, this does not necessarily need to be the case. In reality, much of what I have discussed brings to the forefront the overall importance and power of psychological principles in all aspects of our lives. Understanding the social and psychological dynamics within the workplace is essential for our own well-being and professional growth. In addition, this understanding will help you develop an enriching and rewarding career, one in which you not only help others but also help yourself in the process.

Having said this, it is important to note that my use of the term *wealth* throughout this book can be interpreted many different ways. I see it as a metaphor for those very ideals we seek for our clients: self-awareness, peace, balance, and prosperity.

And in the end, lasting success in any profession comes down to good intentions, integrity, and quality. These sales and marketing concepts will create a lasting impression with clients because of your ability to consistently offer high-quality/value-based services that will add richness to their lives. It is within this realm that true success takes place.

Find opportunities to use some of these principles. Choose those that are in harmony with your value system and philosophical approach. Your ability to customize these approaches within your daily life will lead you on a path to success that you may not have imagined possible.

Good luck and all the best!

Appendix
Business Development
Worksheets and Exercises

MARKETING ACTIVITIES LIST

If you're feeling uninspired or simply have no idea how to begin a marketing campaign, take a look at some of the ideas on this list.

- Build a network by getting yourself out there.
  - Volunteer
  - Join local area boards
  - Offer your expertise to county agencies
  - Participate in fundraising events
- **Leverage your existing network** to help you build partnerships with key referral sources. Who can your friends and colleagues introduce you to?
- **Join mental health social networking sites** and be a valuable contributor (e.g., realmentalhealth.com, webtribes.com).
  - Create a scalable web site.
  - Offer a free resource you developed (e.g., e-book, fact sheet, resource list, research project) and share it with the world.
  - Demystify mental health by creating an online venue for open and honest dialogue.
  - Create a Twitter account and build a following.
  - Use e-mail subscriptions and RSS feeds to capture people who might be interested in what you have to say and offer.
  - Consider a blog instead of a web site.
  - Hire a search engine optimization expert to improve your site's visibility.
  - Offer clients the ability to schedule appointments from your web site.
- **Host a teleseminar or create a podcast.** A great way to build visibility is through sharing your skills and communicating your message using a variety of communication channels.
- **Deliver a training or seminar** and donate 100% of your earnings to a local area mental health initiative.
- **Develop brochures and marketing materials** that answer a customer need.
  - Make them more than just a decoration or a self-serving tool that no one will read.
  - If it all possible, avoid creating marketing materials on your own! Find an expert.
- Remember that frequency and relevance are most important when advertising.

- The frequency with which you advertise in a specific magazine and the relevance of that vehicle is far more important than how many places you choose to advertise in.
- Incorporate a "Call to Action" in all your advertisements and marketing materials.
  - Are you asking potential clients to call for a free consultation or sign up for a free seminar? How do you encourage action and build trust so you earn someone's business?
- Work hard at becoming a true expert at one or two things and know those areas better than anyone!
  - Niche markets rule in today's marketplace.
- Join an online therapist locator service such as Find-A-Therapist.com.
- Post announcements of events you are involved in through **free public domain space** found in local newspapers.
- Define and clarify your mission and your message. Make it compelling!
- Brand yourself effectively based on your mission (e.g., look, feel, approach, values).
- Write articles and post them online.
- Submit your articles on Digg.com and other web sites to build awareness and recognition.
- Build a strong partnership with regional and national **employee assistance programs.**
- **Join local area TV networks as a panel member** or as an expert for public service or wellness initiatives. Local TV stations are always looking for experts.
- **Launch a direct mail campaign to your targeted audience.** This works best if you send mailers out on at least three separate occasions.
- **Launch an online mail campaign. If you do it right, it's free!** Offer free information to your market, get noticed, and ask their permission to join a mailing list. Use this list intelligently to offer ongoing advice.
- **Do the work.** Remember that passion combined with will and commitment wins out.

IDEAS AT THE EDGES

This list, while somewhat similar to the marketing initiatives guide, is intended to get you thinking beyond traditional boundaries. Here are a few items designed to get you out of your head and into a place that motivates and excites you.

- Offer something surprising and unexpected to people at no cost (e.g., a free e-book you wrote, a free consultation, a free workshop).
- Organize a community conference on a specific mental health topic. Invite experts in the community to speak and give them all an opportunity to promote themselves while helping the community in the process.
- Form strategic partnerships with organizations and people so when the time is right you will have enough connections and influence to make big things happen.
- Refer people to your competitors when they would be a better fit. This will impress potential clients and will help build stronger partnerships in the community.
- Lead a movement. Tap into communities that are doing things you are passionate about and create vehicles where the community can share information and connect with one another.
- Start a blog. This is a great way to lead a movement and a great way to build credibility.
- While looking for a job, spend a significant amount of time volunteering for good causes and helping others in general.
- Ask less experienced practitioners with little knowledge of your services for their thoughts on what you are doing.
- Get rid of your web site and start over with something better.
- Find time to learn. E-books and podcasts are great ways to learn and they're usually free! Choose to do this instead of watching TV or listening to the radio.
- Save your money and attend a conference you would have thought to be too expensive.
- Entertain ideas that you initially thought were too crazy to consider.
- Entertain ideas that others think are crazy to consider.
- Change your daily routine. Shake things up!
- Make time for creative and healing endeavors (art projects, yoga, meditation).
- Help people succeed. Do this as often as possible.
- Attend a meeting or gathering you might think has no relevance to the work you do.
- Make an effort to meet people you believe have no connection to what you are doing.
- Find ways to use your clinical skills to cross over to other industries.

MARKETING PLAN COMPONENTS

1. **Find your opportunity.**
    - Research your industry and your markets.
    - Find gaps and niches you can enter.

2. **Brand yourself effectively.**
    - Clarify your strengths.
    - Crystallize your compelling message and your mission.
    - Know your key differentiators. What makes you unique?

3. **Analyze potential markets.**
    - Know your customer.
    - Know how best to reach your customer.

4. **Identify your marketing initiatives.**
    - Choose three or four marketing channels as a starting point.
    - Look for diversity in your initiatives.
    - Stay commited to your plan.

CHANGE THE WAY YOU WORK

Creating An Exercise Program For Your Career

Make an effort to rework your daily routine. Find time for specific mental health activities you enjoy.

How many hours per week can you dedicate to this endeavor? _____

How many days per week? _____

List your most common daily activities other than work
(e.g., watching television, shopping, dinners, social events).

_____

_____

_____

_____

_____

_____

_____

_____

List some alternative activities you can focus on
(e.g., learn a new skill, read psychology books, practice creative thinking exercises, research mental health topics, build networks via social media).

_____

_____

_____

_____

_____

_____

_____

_____

Research shows that if you dedicate a specific number of hours per week and stay committed for up to six months you will position yourself as a leader in your industry. You will be more energized, more knowledgeable and better positioned than 90% of the practitioners in your marketplace. Give it a try!

Bibliography

Beckwith, H. (1997). *Selling the Invisible: A Field Guide to Modern Marketing*. New York: Business Plus.

Carnegie, D. (1981). *How to Win Friends and Influence People* (3rd ed.). New York: Pocket Books.

Cialdini, R. (2007). *Influence: The Psychology of Persuasion*. New York: Harper-Collins.

Frankl, V. (1984). *Man's Search For Meaning* (3rd ed.). New York: Washington Square Press.

Gladwell, M. (2008). *Outliers: The Story of Success*. New York: Little, Brown and Company.

Gitomer, J. (2005). *The Little Red Book of Sales Answers*. New Jersey: Prentice Hall.

Godin, S. (1999). *Permission Marketing: Turning Strangers Into Friends And Friends Into Customers*. New York: Simon & Schuster.

Godin, S. (2006). *Small Is the New Big*. New York: Portfolio.

Levinson, J. C. (2007). *Guerrilla Marketing* (4th ed.). New York: Houghton Mifflin.

Michalko, M. (2006). *Thinkertoys* (2nd ed.). Berkeley, CA: 10 Speed Press

Rumbauskas, F. (2007). *Selling Sucks: How to Stop Selling and Start Getting Prospects to Buy*. Hoboken, NJ: John Wiley & Sons.

REFERENCES

French, J. R. P., Jr., & Raven, B. H. (1959). The bases of social power. In D. Cartwright (Ed.), *Studies in social power* (pp. 150–167). Ann Arbor, MI: Institute for Social Research.

Levine, R., Locke, C., Searls, D., & Weinberg, D. (1999). *The Cluetrain Manifesto*. Retrieved November 18, 2009, from http://www.cluetrain.com.

Milgram S. (1963). Behavioral study of obedience. *Journal of Abnormal Social Psychology, 67*, 371–378.

Raven, B. H. (1992). A power/interaction model of interpersonal influence: French and Raven thirty years later. *Journal of Social Behavior and Personality, 7*(2), 217–244.

Suler, J. (2002). The basic psychological features of cyberspace. In *The Psychology of Cyberspace*, http://www-usr.rider.edu/~suler/psycyber/basicfeat.html.

Suler, J. (2004). The future of online psychotherapy and clinical work. In *The Psychology of Cyberspace*, http://www-usr.rider.edu/~suler/psycyber/futurether.html.

Index

Index